WORRIED SICK

WORRIED SICK

Break Free
from Chronic Worry
to Achieve Mental &
Physical Health

Karol Ward

BERKLEY BOOKS, NEW YORK

THE BERKLEY PUBLISHING GROUP
Published by the Penguin Group
Penguin Group (USA) Inc.
375 Hudson Street, New York, New York 10014, USA
Penguin Group (Canada), 90 Eglinton Avenue East, Suite 700, Toronto, Ontario M4P 2Y3, Canada
(a division of Pearson Penguin Canada Inc.)
Penguin Books Ltd., 80 Strand, London WC2R 0RL, England
Penguin Group Ireland, 25 St. Stephen's Green, Dublin 2, Ireland (a division of Penguin Books Ltd.)
Penguin Group (Australia), 250 Camberwell Road, Camberwell, Victoria 3124, Australia
(a division of Pearson Australia Group Pty. Ltd.)
Penguin Books India Pvt. Ltd., 11 Community Centre, Panchsheel Park, New Delhi—110 017, India
Penguin Group (NZ), 67 Apollo Drive, Rosedale, North Shore 0632, New Zealand
(a division of Pearson New Zealand Ltd.)
Penguin Books (South Africa) (Pty.) Ltd., 24 Sturdee Avenue, Rosebank, Johannesburg 2196,
South Africa

Penguin Books Ltd., Registered Offices: 80 Strand, London WC2R 0RL, England

This book is an original publication of The Berkley Publishing Group.

Copyright © 2010 by Karol Ward.
Interior text design by Tiffany Estreicher.

PRINTING HISTORY
Berkley trade paperback edition / May 2010

Library of Congress Cataloging-in-Publication Data

Ward, Karol.
Worried sick / Karol Ward. — Berkley trade pbk. ed.
    p.   cm.
    ISBN 978-0-425-23411-2
1. Stress (Physiology).   2. Nutrition.   3. Mind and body.   I. Title.
QP82.2.S8W36 2010
612.3—dc22   2010001850

PRINTED IN THE UNITED STATES OF AMERICA

10   9   8   7   6   5   4   3   2   1

*This book is dedicated to my brother Patrick,
who has provided me with support, comfort, and insight
as we walked a very special journey together.*

WORRIED SICK

ACKNOWLEDGMENTS

I want to thank the many people who provided such wonderful opportunity and support for the creation of this book.

Thanks to my editor, Andie Avila at Berkley Publishing, for her enthusiasm about the topic, her support for my ideas, and her ability to focus my writing by asking great questions. Thank you to my agent, Sharon Bowers from the Miller Agency, for her ability to make the creation of this book an authentic process.

Many thanks and lots of love to my husband and support, Michael Souveroff, who believes in me without question and makes me laugh when I need to the most.

A huge thank-you goes to Sylvia Moritz, my friend and second set of eyes. Thank you for your time and willingness to read those first drafts. I very much appreciate your feedback, encouragement, and great advice on the use of images.

I want to acknowledge my mother, Dorothy Ward, who has faced a very tough time with remarkable courage.

Acknowledgments

For Jesse Klein, who has provided caring and support for my mother during this time. Thank you so much, Jesse.

I want to acknowledge my niece Miranda, whose presence in my life brings me great happiness.

I want to thank my brother David, who always wanted to know how the book was coming along and share his enthusiasm for my success. Thanks, Dave.

I want acknowledge my brother Charlie, for the strength he has had to make big changes in his life.

I want to thank all the experts who contributed to my book: Amy Torres, Rochelle Rice, Jeanette Bronee, Leigh Hansen, Jane Burbank, Kelly Brogan, Tina Felluss, Tara Keegan, Wendy Flynn, and Martha McKittrick. What a powerful group of wise and intelligent women. The information you gave me was supportive and thoughtful, and you all understood the importance of this subject.

Of course, thank you to my many patients and clients who have inspired me with their courage to face their fears and claim their joy so that they can live the lives they want. The journey of self-examination is not easy, and those who undertake it are to be acknowledged for their willingness to take even the first step.

CONTENTS

INTRODUCTION

My psychotherapy colleagues and I share a saying that goes, "You give a session; you get a session." What we mean is that often the exact same issue our patients show up to talk about in their session is the very thing we end up looking at within ourselves later. This phenomenon does not happen all the time, but it can—mainly when the timing is right and we as therapists are open to facing something we need to understand about ourselves. We seem to get presented with the opportunity to learn from the very people we are trying to help. And through the course of that interaction, we heal what we need to.

Surprisingly, as I wrote *Worried Sick*, I was presented with an opportunity to tackle my own worries and learn to heal them. What I did not already know on the subject of worry was presented to me in the guise of my mother's deteriorating health. About six months before I started this book project, my mother, a once private and independent woman, began to falter first physically and then mentally. In the course of what seemed like a few months, she became frail and searched for words that eluded her. Her mind, once sharp with facts about history, geography, and genealogy, became fragmented. Her balance, appetite, and ability to remember conversations from earlier that same day were severely affected. My brother Patrick and I became very worried about her ability to care for herself, and I arranged for a full neuropsychological evaluation. When she was finally given a diagnosis, it was determined that she had a combination of early-onset Alzheimer's and vascular dementia.

I can still remember when I read the first page of my mother's very detailed medical report. I had a hard time focusing on the words and what they meant. The terminology was clinical though understandable, but it was information I just couldn't process because I simply was not ready for it. I think I went into a minor state of shock, if shock ever can be minor, and then drifted into a place of denial. I know my mind was registering the information on some level while my body slid into numbness. After I read everything, I took a breath, sat down on the couch in the doctor's office, and asked myself, "How can I possibly handle this? And how can I help my mom handle this?"

What was most difficult for me and my family, and especially for my mother, was the fact that she knew she was unable to remember things like she used to. Because the disease had already progressed, she did not fully comprehend what was wrong with her, but she was aware that something was. After the diagnosis, it became our job to guide her so that she didn't lose her way in the day-to-day living of her life. At one point, after having an unexpected fall, she said to me, "I need you to watch out for me." I told her I would take care of her and she should not worry. I, on the other hand, found out over time that I would do plenty of worrying for the both of us.

I worried about keeping my mother safe so that she could retain her dignity and have some independence. I wondered how I would balance my own life between taking care of her and maintaining my career. In caring for my mom, I was challenged as a daughter, a woman, and a therapist. I found that becoming my mother's caregiver forced me to rely on all the skills I had learned in my practice—I found myself working around the clock. Everything I had used in the past to counsel and comfort my patients was put into use over and over again with my mom. I listened to her fears and tried to teach her some tools for coping, such as asking for help and taking care of her body. I met with her and her doctor so that she understood the course of medical treatment. We talked about how she could exercise, talk to a counselor if needed, and make changes in her diet. We discussed the importance of staying connected to her community and keeping her mind stimulated through reading and music, both of which gave her great pleasure. It was difficult at times to be in the role of parent and yet long for my mother to reassure me that everything would be all right—something she could not do. It was also a struggle to watch the familiar become unfamiliar and have the ground shift daily. My mother's love of driving could no longer be part of her life, and her ability to play bridge with friends was gone because she could not remember what other players had bid. Also, though my mother was aware of her current surroundings and the people near her, she was unable to recall significant events from six months earlier, even when prompted—events such as a family gathering or hospital stay of a few weeks.

Many of you have faced similar situations—caring for ailing parents or a sick child or facing the loss of a secure job. And though we imagine ourselves to be strong and resilient, nothing prepares you for the kind of instability, stress, and worry that come with such particular issues. You feel tired, drained, and restless. You stay awake at night thinking about what you can do to make it better, and you face the next day with exhaustion. Then during the day you struggle to keep your focus with your job, your children, and a variety of daily responsibilities. You want to be present for all of these things, but you find yourself tired and distracted. Your body feels tense and you notice that you have a chronic backache, neck ache, or headache, all due to your worry. You may find yourself with an uneasy stomach, unable to eat or eating too much. Overall, your body feels out of sorts, off balance, and you long for a moment of quiet and peace.

I suspect many of you know what I am talking about—not because you've encountered my exact situation before, but because you may be juggling your own issues such as health concerns, caring for a loved one, or navigating a new career. You could be struggling to hold on to your home or relationship and fear you won't be able to. You may feel overstimulated or overextended, with everyone seeming to need your attention and everything pulling you in a different direction. From what I have witnessed as a therapist, friend, and neighbor, it seems that we all have our arms filled with the worries that life tends to present to us.

With all this going on, it can be perfectly natural, if not helpful, to allow ourselves to worry or to share worries at different times in our lives. However, I've also seen how worrying can be disruptive to our day-to-day functioning. I've seen it with my patients, friends, and colleagues. I certainly have lived through it myself while taking care of my mom in those early days of her diagnosis, before I wrote this book. Whether your worries are chronic, in the moment, caused by outside events, or created by your own imagination, constant worry does eventually erode the quality of your life. What I'm talking about is the kind of worry that is relentless, overwhelming, and eventually debilitating—the kind of worry that interrupts your life and affects how you live day to day. It's the type of worry that influences how you perceive yourself, the world around you, and your ability to make effective, healthy decisions.

Healthy decisions are important to our well-being and are easy to implement. The mind-body connection is a powerful thing, and our thoughts can challenge our physical well-being. Conversely, when that connection is flowing, our ability to face our difficulties becomes stronger when we take care of our mind, body, and spirit. If we are mindful of this connection and do our best to take care of ourselves, we do not get bowled over so easily by what we are worried about. The more we learn about the different types of worry, why worry shows up, how we are affected, and what to do, the more we lessen worry's hold on us. With this knowledge, we will be able to keep our perspective, make decisions about what we need, and educate ourselves about ongoing self-care. Instead of feeling at the mercy of worry, we learn to take charge when it appears so that we do not get caught in its grip. And once we break free of unnecessary worry, we can finally start living.

Worried Sick is about understanding the many aspects of worry and finding ways to support ourselves so that worry does not take over our lives. Being worried affects not just our mind but also our body and spirit. Our health, ability to cope, and outlook can be severely compromised when worry becomes a dominating force. Worry may always be a part of the human experience, but it does not have to be center stage all the time. There are tools and techniques to keep worry from stealing so much of our time and energy while we are trying to live life. We all have enough going on without having to get caught in worry's web. From where I stand, we need and can find many methods to keep ourselves afloat during difficult times.

Worried Sick addresses how excessive worry affects our mental, physical, and emotional health. In the first three chapters, we will look at how and why worry shows up. We'll start here because the more you understand the roots and triggers of worry, the more you will be able to manage it as you go along. As on any journey, once you know your starting point, you can plan what you will need to do for the rest of your trip. Also, understanding the complexity of worry will help you uncover certain patterns of behavior. As you read Part 1, you may discover some surprising causes for your worry, even though most of us feel that worry is an unexpected and uninvited guest in our minds. You will learn to connect the dots between where your worry originates and how it shows up. In looking at the different origins, I'll discuss how worry isn't always the result of something happening in the present, but that it can have ties to the past.

In Part 2, we look at different strategies that you can use to stay worry-free, including important information on self-care. You will see how movement, nutrition, and sleep are keys to feeling centered and calm. And you'll learn simple techniques to ease your anxiety so that you can better overcome your worries and lead a healthier life.

Throughout this book, I will be presenting stories of real people and how they have been affected by worry. I have changed their names and any details that would reveal their identities, but the stories are true. Along with my own story, I'll share the journeys of others, which will highlight the impact of worry and illustrate how worry can be managed. I have also included the advice of trusted experts who have developed effective methods for dealing with the physical and behavioral impact of worry. Their contributions show that you can take many approaches to keep worry from making you ill, and you get to choose what works for you. Once you discover how you get stuck in a particular kind of worrying, you can consciously choose a strategy to help you let go of it. You may even find that one method helps you deal with one worry, whereas another strategy may be just what you need to manage another. Take the time to find out what you need to learn most about yourself and worry in your life.

What I have learned about how to maintain my balance while facing deep worry is something I will never forget, and it's something I want to pass along to you. I could not have realized the unexpected capacity we have as human beings to care for others and to persevere under the most difficult circumstances. Most important, I learned that we can manage, defuse, or endure all types of worry when we have the support and tools available. That is one of the strongest lessons I have learned from my experiences with my mother—we cannot control what happens to us, but we can control how we choose to react to what happens to us. We can worry our lives away or accept what is and find resources to help us move through it. I wish this lesson did not have to show up the way it did, but we usually do not get to choose when and how difficulties enter our lives. I invite you to take a journey with me and learn that you, too, can heal your chronic worry and take charge of your life.

Part 1

CHAPTER ONE

The Fundamentals of Worry

Who can say that in their life they have not spent time worrying about one thing or another? We may experience worry to varying degrees, but we all seem to be focused on and preoccupied with our own set of issues and how we will be affected by the outcome. Personal finance, the economy, our health, our aging parents' health, getting on the highway, getting on a plane, seeing family, or not seeing them enough—there's plenty we seem to be concerned about. Most people I spoke to about my book were eager to let me know about the many things that cause them worry. My friend Rene even asked to be my first case study: "You're writing about worry? Let me volunteer. You can write about my life and everything I worry about. You could fill two, maybe three books because there's not much I don't worry about!" She laughed as she said it, but in her humor lies a real truth. Rene worries a lot, and though it hasn't impacted her physical and emotional well-being, I honestly believe that it's only a matter of time.

Worry affects our bodies as well as our minds. Yet many of us don't often consider the mind-body connection and how the troublesome thoughts we hold in our minds can affect our bodies and behavior. Think about it. How many times have you developed an upset stomach after a performance review or gotten a splitting headache when you tried to figure out how you were going to make ends meet when doing the family budget? Our bodies react to what our minds are processing, and if there is a lot of worry going on, our bodies will feel the impact. Why does that happen? It happens because a physical adjustment occurs in our bodies in response to worry, a shifting that happens both inside and out. We often do this adjusting to prevent or avoid fueling the worry, fear, or anxiety that is making us uncomfortable. On the inside we try to "handle" those emotions in both our mind and body so that we can feel more in control. We may do things like hold our breath, lock the back of our knees, tighten our shoulders, or clamp down on our jaws to manage the stress we are experiencing. As time goes by, this way of protecting ourselves from uncomfortable feelings becomes so much a part of us that we do not even realize we are doing it or how it is affecting us. We are no longer aware that we are storing our worry in our tight shoulders, back, or neck because we have gotten used to handling it that way. We do not usually realize the toll it takes on us until it shows up as physical pain, and that often is our first clue that worry has taken hold of us.

Another way people handle their worry is by choosing behaviors that ultimately turn out to be destructive. They turn outward and become trapped in patterns of overeating, overworking, and overspending, which ultimately provide only temporary relief. In order to alleviate their internal anxiety, they seek excess food, alcohol, or shopping but end up feeling worse. The poor food choices, alcohol consumption, and stacks of bills only end up compounding whatever stress they are feeling, and then there are more things to worry about. The more we act out this way, the worse we can end up feeling.

Worry and Stress

Worry also has a well-known partner in crime known as stress. Stress is most commonly defined as "an applied force or system of forces that tends to strain or deform a body." That is a pretty explicit description of what stress can do to us—both physically and mentally. Many times the culprit for causing that strain is none other than worry. Worry is a major catalyst for stress, and we all know what it is like to feel the overall tension associated with the stress we have in our lives. In fact, stress has become the familiar way we describe our lives because it is the perfect word to capture everything we are juggling. When people ask us how we are, we say, "Oh, I am so stressed," or "Work is so stressful," or "The kids are stressing me out!" But it's not stress acting alone. Worry is often behind that stress, and together they have become the king and queen of the castle and can rule our lives with an iron fist.

Different Types of Worry

CIRCUMSTANTIAL WORRY

Some things that we worry about preoccupy our minds because they require our attention. We may be worried because we have project deadlines to meet at work, we are looking for a job, or we are trying to downsize and sell our home. It's natural to worry about the application process when applying to a school, or about the pregnancy and labor when expecting a baby, or what to study and how well you'll retain information for the bar exam. Many moments, experiences, and situations in life demand our attention and cause us to worry. We worry about those issues because the results matter to us—and what we do or say can have an impact on the outcome. We worry that we won't get things right or that we'll do something wrong.

In these situations, though, it's likely that once you have completed a process or arrived at a resolution, you're done worrying. Worries that are concrete and that we can manage because they have a beginning and an end are circumstantial worries. For example, once an assignment has been turned in to a teacher, your job is done and you don't have to worry about making the deadline. Once you've been approved for a mortgage, you can stop worrying about whether you will ever own your first home. In these situations, nothing is left for you to worry about because you've ultimately done everything within your control.

Sometimes, though, our circumstantial worry is hard to

perceive logically. We may have a nagging feeling in the pit of our stomach that something is wrong or off with a person or situation, but we can't quite put our finger on it. This is usually where our instinct comes into play. Instinct is our built-in biological system of self-care that helps us decide whether something feels either good or bad or is safe, such as whether you should walk down that dark street or choose another path. Years ago I worked with a patient who was in the process of buying a house with his partner. Even though he felt the house they wanted was a good deal, something about the process was causing my patient to worry. "It's not going smoothly, and I'm picking up weird vibes from the owners," he told me. When I asked him what he meant, he said, "They are really eager to sell, but I feel there is something they are keeping from us. They just seem really nervous, and it doesn't make sense because the house is beautiful and in a great location. It's making us worry about the seller's motivation." Ultimately my patient decided against the house, and a few months later he found out that another house was going to be built quite close to the property line. This information had not been revealed by the sellers and would have left my patient and his partner with no legal recourse because the new home would have technically not been on their land. My patient's worry, led by his gut instinct's reaction to the sellers, signaled to him that something was off in this seemingly great house deal.

In a July 2009 article in the *New York Times* on brain power and hunches, a Princeton University study noted "how a gut feeling may arise before a person becomes conscious of what the brain has registered." This article illustrates that we sense things before we become consciously aware of exactly what we are feeling. If we find that this worry goes away once we have made a decision, completed a task or assignment, or arrived at a resolution, then we've encountered another type of circumstantial worry—one that we resolve through trusting our instinct.

Because these kinds of worries grab our attention but do not dominate our quality of life, we can consider circumstantial worry natural, if not healthy. Chronic worry, however, is a different story.

CHRONIC WORRY

Worry's power and the impact it has on our minds and bodies have been in the news quite often over the last few years. Many medical and health practitioners acknowledge that stress caused by worry takes a toll on the human body. Stress-related worry affects us not only physically, but also emotionally. After all, when we are worried, the range of emotional reactions we have runs the gamut. We feel sad, angry, and fearful. Sometimes our mood takes a more serious dip, and we end up feeling depressed and anxious. If these feelings are not resolved and released, they could lead to illness.

For me, constant worry is like having your car get stuck in the mud. The more fuel you give the engine, the more the tires keep spinning and spinning. You keep pumping the gas pedal in order to break free, but you cannot seem to move forward. Having chronic worry is similar to those muddy tires. When our mental and physical health is affected by chronic worry, it causes us to feel trapped and out of control. Our minds want solutions, yet our bodies become too tense in reaction to our worry and can't help with the process. Sometimes that tension shows up as a jittery, can't-sit-still feeling. Other times it feels like we have been hit by a truck and just can't muster up the energy to move, let alone think. Whatever our physical reaction, it's hard to think clearly while it's going on. Both our bodies and minds are trying to handle it but appear to be at cross purposes. Until we can figure out ways to get ourselves unstuck from worry's hold, we remain in a state of mental and physical spinning.

I know from experience that the brain affects the body and the body affects the brain. When we are feeling clear and focused in our minds, we usually have more vitality in our bodies. When we are physically healthy, we usually have more energy available to us to figure out solutions. Yet when these two areas are off balance because of worry, they have an effect on each other. We worry about our kids and find ourselves with a headache at the end of the day. We become physically tense during a stressful, busy morning at work and find we can't concentrate for the rest of the afternoon. Even if we are not conscious of it, the interplay between our body and mind is constantly happening. However, when worry becomes chronic, without giving us a break, we will feel it on many different levels.

In his article "The Power of Mood," Michael D. Lemonick observed, "The chronic stress that millions of people feel from simply trying to deal with the pressures of modern life can unleash a flood of hormones that are useful in the short term but subtly toxic if they persist" (*Time*, 2003). The stress he mentions can show up as illness that occurs in the mind and also as illness that affects the body. We are all starting to notice this. According to the American Psychological Association, "80 percent of Americans say that during the past few years they have become more aware of how their mental health and emotions can affect their health."

What this is saying is that as the volume of stress and worry increases over time in our lives, we feel the *physical* impact on a daily basis. We feel it not only directly through nervousness, tension, and agitation but indirectly as well through some of the unhealthy choices we make to cope. A terrible cycle is created between worry and the symptoms it produces, such as sleep problems, poor nutrition, mental anxiety, and the deterioration of our physical health. When we are chronically worried, as we can see from the preceding studies, we don't function as well. We need to find ways to give ourselves a break from our current worries and, for some, worries that haven't even occurred.

The remarkable thing about chronic worry is that our bodies and minds cannot really tell whether the worry is *real* or *imagined*. When we worry over the possibility of bad things happening even though they have not even occurred, it is called *future tripping*. Future tripping happens when we read things online or in the paper or watch the news and hear predictions about bad events that *may* occur but haven't yet. It's the kind of news that stimulates our anxiety because we feel it hanging over us. This has occurred quite a bit with stories about potential cyber attacks or possible terrorist threats. We feel held hostage by the possibility of these events even though we may not have a personal connection to them. Even without the connection, such possibilities can have the same impact as if we were intimately involved in one of those situations.

An example of future tripping is a circumstance like the following. Let's say during the summer you read in the paper that it may be a bad winter in your area. Not as scary as our other scenarios but still something that could affect you. If you start to future trip about the possibility of a hard winter, you find yourself worrying about how you will get to work when it's snowing, and then what would happen if you slipped on the ice, broke your ankle, and couldn't make it to work. Then you worry about how your bills would get paid and whether you could pay rent. The next thing you know, you are feeling stressed, your heart is pounding, and your stomach is churning with anxiety, and it's only July. Your body and mind can't tell the difference. They simply react to what information is absorbed and respond accordingly.

What helps with future tripping is preparation and solid information. When you hear or read something that scares you, knowing what you need to be ready and validating the source will give you comfort. If you feel you need to have certain items on hand in your house to help you feel secure, such as a to-go bag or extra supplies such as food, wood, or heating oil, then take care of that. If you want more information about a certain topic that concerns you, then research that topic and find out what you need to know so that you are informed. Go to good sources of information, such as trusted websites, libraries, or official local and national government offices, or speak with friends and colleagues whose opinions you trust. Then do your best to prepare with the information you receive, and let go of what you can't control. Use what you learn to empower you and not overwhelm you.

Are You Worrying More Than You Need To?

Let's take a look. Answer the following questions with either yes or no.

Do you have difficulty falling asleep?

❏ Yes

❏ No

Do you feel overwhelmed or frustrated by events in your life?

❏ Yes

❏ No

Are you preoccupied with the problems of friends and family?

❏ Yes

❏ No

Do you have high blood pressure?

❏ Yes

❏ No

Do you create time to relax during the week or on the weekend?

- ❑ Yes
- ❑ No

Do you have any stomach problems (acid reflux, indigestion, bloating, diarrhea, or constipation)?

- ❑ Yes
- ❑ No

Do you feel stressed most of the time?

- ❑ Yes
- ❑ No

Do you exercise or move on a regular basis?

- ❑ Yes
- ❑ No

Do you feel that your mood is affected by outside events in your life?

- ❑ Yes
- ❑ No

Do you feel distracted and unable to concentrate?

- ❑ Yes
- ❑ No

If you have more "yes" answers than "no" answers, chances are you are being affected by constant worry. Whether the worry is your own or someone else's, it is time to free yourself from the trap.

Falling into a Worry Trap

My friend Sharon was a generally energetic and lively person. A successful saleswoman living in Manhattan and with her own business, she had always had a busy work schedule and a full social life. However, a few years ago, the economic climate of the sales industry changed. Companies began to cut back and were not as free with their spending. Despite this, Sharon continued to stay afloat financially but found she was developing a problem going to sleep at night. Usually a sound sleeper, she noticed it was taking her longer to fall asleep, and then she was able to sleep for only a couple of hours. As a result, Sharon woke up tired and groggy but of course felt compelled to put energy into her business. A vicious pattern began to emerge, and it went on for many months. The more Sharon tried to keep her business going, the more her sleep was affected. The more her sleep was affected, the more she worried about keeping her business healthy. In fact, her concern about her business was what triggered her sleep problems in the first place, though she initially did not connect the two. After all, she was still successful and was able to handle her daily living expenses. Sharon initially thought her struggle with sleep was a separate issue on its own, but she soon discovered that her low-grade worry about her career was directly connected to her insomnia. We will discuss her exploration and ultimate solution to her sleep problem later in the book, but her dilemma is fairly universal. I have observed that the impact of worry often shows up as a specific symptom.

One of the most common things I hear when worried people come into my office is that they feel helpless concerning whatever they are worried about. In those moments, the emotions and energy of worry cloud their perspective. It consumes them and occupies their mind. The worry could be a low-grade one about their future career, the economy, or their ability to find love. Or the worry could be large and looming, concerning the health of a loved one or the potential loss of their home. No matter how big or small the worry actually is, the fact that it is a concern to the person experiencing it is what makes it important.

As I mentioned, one of the underlying threads that all worriers seem to share is that of powerlessness. Worriers feel powerless to change the issues and situations that surround them. Sometimes that powerlessness is real because their current reality is one that they cannot change. They are stuck at a job that requires them to commute long hours but cannot imagine leaving because of the real financial responsibilities of taking care of their family. Sometimes the powerlessness is false; they actually do have the tools to change a worrisome situation but in the moment are too confused to know what to do. Perhaps they know that the romantic relationship they are in is not working, and they are not stuck for any other reason but their inability at this time to find the emotional strength to leave. However, with most people it seems that all the mulling over and thinking about their situation does not make it better. Excess worrying does not usually shift our mood and help us feel more upbeat. Most times, we feel worse! We end up scaring ourselves with worst-case scenarios while the worrying continues to erode our ability to see things in context and perspective. We do not want to get stuck in the worry trap, and in order to escape it, we need information and strategies. The more we arm ourselves with the knowledge of how we respond to worry in our bodies and minds, the better we can deal with it. As you continue reading, you will learn to identify the symptoms, differentiate between the different types of worry, and apply the different strategies, which will help you feel more empowered.

The Body and the Worry Process

Fight or Flight

As we have seen, we respond with our whole being whether a worrisome situation is actually happening or we *anticipate* it happening. When we do, this causes a physiological response, which is the way our organs, tissues, and cells function together as soon as we become stressed. Our bodies react and go into fight-or-flight mode. The *fight-or-flight response* is probably something you have experienced before. That's the rush of energy you feel when you are confronted with a potential danger; it enables you to stand your ground or head for the hills. It is the reaction you have when you hear news about a friend or family member that concerns you. It's the kind of response you have when you hear a bad economic forecast. Whether the situation you are responding to is real or only a possibility does not seem to matter. Your heart rate speeds up, your skin becomes flushed or clammy, and your lips and throat feel dry. All of these reactions are stress responses and, as we have seen, worry definitely feeds our stress.

Imagine, then, if you were in a constant state of worry. On some level those physical fight-or-flight reactions would continue to happen. You would be constantly expending energy, your body would be in a perpetual state of alertness, and there would be no opportunity to calm down. Dr. Jonathan Steinberg, who led a study on heart arrhythmias (abnormal heart rhythms) after September 11, 2001, observed, "Prolonged stress has physiological consequences." Because many people were in emotional shock and reeling from the attacks, they continued to feel the effect for a period of time afterward. As Dr. Steinberg noted, over time the energy of worry and stress drains both the body and the mind.

SYMPATHETIC NERVOUS SYSTEM

When we respond to something that we perceive as dangerous or unsafe, our sympathetic nervous system kicks in. A helpful way to remember how the sympathetic nervous system works is to remember that it contains the word *sympathy*. The term reminds me of our own response to something that someone shares with us that we have also experienced. We feel sympathetic and understanding because we can relate to their situation. Therefore, I think of our nervous system as having a sympathetic response to what we are concerned about and then having a series of reactions. Those reactions are all the physical symptoms I described earlier as our bodies respond to real or imagined danger.

PARASYMPATHETIC NERVOUS SYSTEM

After we sense that a worrisome situation is not as bad as we first imagined, our parasympathetic nervous system takes over and helps us move from panic to calm. The prefix *para-* means "to accompany or assist, to work alongside." So after our initial anxious reaction, in which our sympathetic nervous system is activated, the parasympathetic nervous system takes over for the sympathetic nervous system, whose job is now done. It is amazing that our bodies have these physiological systems to help us weather all sorts of storms. The more we know how to maintain those systems, the better we can handle all sorts of taxing situations.

Whenever I want to visualize how these two systems work to keep us in balance, I use a particular image. The image of a roller coaster perfectly captures how we respond on an emotional and physical level to a variety of situations in life. I feel that it effectively describes what happens to us when we allow ourselves to go with the flow of our sympathetic and parasympathetic nervous systems. I want you to picture the biggest roller coaster you have ever seen or been on and think about the very first hill—the one at the beginning and usually one of the tallest.

Now imagine yourself taking a ride on that roller coaster. Even if you have never actually been on such a ride, you probably have watched many people go on them and seen their response. See yourself going up that first steep hill, knowing you will be going over the top in a few moments. Usually at this point in the ride people feel a combination of tremendous excitement and fear. Those emotions build and become more intense as the roller coaster takes you toward the highest part of the hill. Suddenly you are at the top, and before you know it, you are hurtling down the other side, picking up more and more speed as you move downward. You find yourself yelling with joy, fear, and maybe even relief as you fly to the bottom. When you get there, if that was the end of the ride, your car slowly comes to a halt. You probably feel your body slowing down as well, until you are calmer.

A roller-coaster ride is a good way to imagine what it is like when we respond and release our emotions. Our feelings build in intensity, just like that first hill, and peak when we reach the height of our feelings, eventually to move into a state of calmness. Of course, emotional reactions happen at different speeds and vary in length, but the healthy release of emotions basically follows the same path. But what happens if those feelings do not get released and, like a chronic state of worry, just keep looping around and around? Well, our emotions do not just fade away. We either find ways to distract ourselves or let them consume our attention every waking moment. We hold all that worry and stress in our bodies, and eventually psychological, physical, and behavioral symptoms start to appear. The worry ride continues whether we want it to or not. How does that occur?

AMYGDALA

Research on worry and the brain shows that the amygdala, which is a small part of the brain located in the center of the head, is a key player in reacting to stress. The amygdala is the most primitive part of the brain and is the area where we "feel" threats or lust first before our higher brain functions join in. Once this area of the brain is activated, it puts the body on high alert. Our senses become sharper, and we very quickly go through an assessment of whether what we are responding to is an immediate threat. So our primitive brain serves a good purpose and sets in motion the fight-or-flight pattern we looked at earlier. However, if we remain in a constant state of mini-crisis, our memory and ability to reason things out for ourselves becomes affected. The motor keeps running, and eventually there is wear and tear on the engine. The more we can access resources that are within, such as working with our body to help release stress and calm down, or without, such as eliminating time-wasting activities and people from our schedule, the better we can find clarity and the ability to cope.

This book will look at the different ways to cope with worry from many perspectives. I want to provide you with both "getting prepared" and "in the moment" techniques to handle your worry. I want to help you shift worry and your response to it from reactive to proactive. In fact, I'm reminded of what one of my workshop participants said to me in regard to chronic worry. She said, "Worry is like trying to open your umbrella when the rain is pouring down and the wind is blowing in your face. When you are in it, you feel both the struggle and stress of trying to figure out the answer." Well, what I have discovered is that the best time to open your umbrella is when you see the clouds forming or the drops are just starting to fall.

Approaching Worry Through Body, Mind, and Spirit

We will be addressing worry throughout this book using a three-tiered approach: body, mind, and spirit. In using this three-tiered method, you'll focus on the various areas to help you unhook from your worrisome thinking. The reason we will look at each of these areas is that they are all affected by worry in their own way. Sometimes your body feels it more through physical symptoms, such as a headache or upset stomach. Other times it will be your mind that gets caught in an endless loop of anxious thinking and ends up fearing the worst. Or maybe it will be your spirit that feels the impact and you end up feeling discouraged, dissatisfied, and blue. As you work on each area individually, you will see how they are all intercon-

BODY
Physical symptoms can include headaches, tight shoulders, upset stomach, or general tension.

MIND
Cluttered thinking and the inability to find answers is caused by chronic worry.

The Three Tiers
The three tiers are interrelated, and stress in one area impacts the others.

SPIRIT
This tier is about how we view our life; worry may cause us not to see the light or make us lose our sense of hope.

nected. When we are physically uptight, we cannot think clearly and we find ourselves confused. When we are mentally churned up, it causes us to feel nervous and tense in our bodies. When our spirits are deflated, our perspective on the world and how we view our future becomes distorted—three separate areas, yet all powerfully interconnected.

Once you understand how you are being impacted by worry, you will be able to choose the method that works for you. One day you may focus on using a method to help your body release its reaction to worry. Another day you will work with your mind and help it move toward clarity, and on another you will alleviate your mood by attending to your spirit. You may find yourself gravitating toward one strategy or another, depending on what you need. If you find yourself with physical symptoms such as muscle tension, upset stomach, or exhaustion, you may want to address how to relax or recharge your body first. If you find yourself thinking the same things over and over but getting no answers, you may want to use a method that gives your mind a break. If you generally feel that your outlook and attitude toward life are negative and uninspired, you may want to choose a technique that lifts your spirit.

As you will see, your overall approach to reducing worry's effect in your life will start with what you need, not what you should be doing. Maybe you find yourself eating too much every afternoon because you are nervous about money and bills. You know you should be eating better but find it impossible to do. You understand the health consequences but are unable to give up your cookie habit. Using an inside-out approach allows you to address what is associated with that need for those afternoon cookies. If you explore what the sugar in the cookies does for you and your worry, you could choose some other way to fill that need. Maybe eating sugar provides you with energy, and if you can find other ways to feel energized, you will be more likely to cut out the junk food. When you address the need, you are more likely to change behavior because you are working from the inside out. That is why I wanted to keep the topic of worry from being yet another thing we have to *think* about. Though I will suggest exercises and offer information, I want the focus of this book to be on you as a whole person. Whether you choose to work on your mind first and then your body, or work on spirit and then your mind, doesn't matter—because working on one area will benefit the others. When these three elements operate together, you will have access to more intellectual, intuitive, and emotional information working together to help you make better decisions about the life you want to lead. These insights will help you feel less burdened by worry.

Body

Looking at things from the inside out means you invest the time to find out more about who you are and what you need. As you begin to pay attention to what your body is telling you about your worry, you will be able to translate what those symptoms mean. Why is your neck tense, or why are your shoulders aching? Where did that headache come from, and why are you struggling with sleep? What would it feel like to take time to calm down and relax? Questions like these will help you discover what you need to reconnect with and revitalize your body.

Mind

When your mind has a chance to unwind, you will experience the difference between feeling as if there are no answers and finding the solution that is right for you. I have seen many patients start their sessions in a state of upset and confusion because they are worried and do not believe they can find answers. Yet creating the time to sort through and work on the issues they have been struggling with usually helps them find solutions. Once you have the space to focus, you too can explore what is blocking you from understanding your worries. Then your mind can shift from fear to insight.

Spirit

You are also able to cope more easily with what life presents to you when your spirit feels lighter. I define *spirit* as our general mood and ability to trust that things can and will work out. How we engage our spirit is unique to each of us. Some of us choose psychological support; others turn to their religious beliefs. Many seek solace in meditation, philosophy, prayer, or quiet reflection. Whatever your choice, as long as you feel that your spirits are lifted and you are able to persevere in your life's journey, you are in the right place.

When we put energy back into our systems, release mental tension, and find an inner balance, we are able to face the world again. Time and time again, we need to physically, intellectually, and spiritually recharge our batteries. When we do so, we reduce our stress, alleviate our confusion, and support our decision-making abilities. Now let us look at the best way to achieve this by applying the Three Cs.

The Three Cs

The Three Cs are three areas that when explored are very effective for managing your worry. They not only incorporate your body, mind, and spirit, but also give you ideas and strategies for keeping worry from taking over. (At the end of each chapter, you will find the Three Cs.) As you read each chapter and work with these three sections, either individually or together, you will find strategies to keep yourself from becoming worried sick.

Calmness

Moving from agitation to calmness will be a great tool for you to use in managing worry. Getting calm means consciously releasing physical and mental tension. You can learn to do this through a variety of exercises and methods found in this book. You know how it feels when you approach issues from a place of either composure or nervousness, and there is a big difference between feeling frantic and feeling in charge. The more you can operate from a place of calm, the better your overall decisions will be.

Now, getting calm does not mean that everything we worry about simply disappears. That is not realistic because many of you are handling ongoing troublesome situations. What it does mean is that as we eliminate chronic overthinking of our situation, we give our minds a break and are able to approach our problems with more confidence. When we are relaxed and calm, we have more control over our daily choices. We are able to access all the internal reserves of information that we need because we are not physically bottled up with worry. As you explore the different chapters of this book, you will see how releasing physical and mental tension leads you from turbulence to tranquility.

Clarity

The mental clutter we experience in today's world is just amazing. Our attention is pulled in many different directions. Everywhere we look, information is being conveyed to us. We are bombarded with news headlines, e-mails, and texts before we even are through with our first cup of coffee. This boosts our anxiety level because we have had little time to process what we are receiving. Getting control over this information overload plus finding the root of what is triggering your worry will mean developing and using the power of choice. Your ability to use your discretion about what you read, watch, and pay attention to will be very important. This could not have been clearer to me than right after the attacks on the World Trade Center.

Back in September 2001 my private-practice office was located in downtown Manhattan, and I had a number of patients who worked and lived near the Financial District. When the World Trade Center towers were attacked, their lives, like many others, were turned upside down. Some of my patients lost friends who worked in the buildings, while others had to run through the streets to escape as the buildings came down. The impact on their lives was far-reaching and caused an excessive amount of continuing and constant worry. Even my patients who had not been directly affected were in a state of anxiety.

As time went on, I paid careful attention to who was able to process the events and who was not. I discovered that the worry and anxiety of some of my patients was being amplified by excessive watching of news. Because of this, I often suggested that the person stop watching so much television news. I assured them that if there was new information of significance, they would be able to find out. But for now, in addition to working through their grief, I recommended they take a much-needed break from the ongoing media coverage. This suggestion calmed many of my patients down and allowed them to function better in their day-to-day lives. They needed to lower their anxiety level in order to process the extraordinary tragedy they had witnessed. I have found that when your view of the world is controlled by the outside, it is vitally important to take back control. Granting my patients the permission they needed to stop watching the news allowed them to feel more in control.

Everyone needs a break once in a while, and sometimes more than we realize. I know when my level of worry is getting the best of me. I usually have to find a way to shut off the part of my mind that is caught in a loop of worry or give it something else to focus on. Maybe I play a game on the computer, read a magazine, or watch a lighthearted television show. Whatever distraction I choose is a conscious effort to interrupt the part of my mind that is caught up with worry. Later on, we will look at additional tools you can use to achieve more mental clarity.

Community

Sharing the burdens of worry is a transformative experience. I use the word *community* to encompass all the resources that are available to us when we are worried sick. Close friends, family members, health practitioners, therapeutic professionals, and spiritual advisers are all there for us to lean on when we need support. Allowing others to share our troubles can bring great emotional comfort. Sometimes we just need to be heard, and that is enough. At other times, we may need more specific advice and guidance that will provide a road map for us to continue forward.

How do we know when we need either community or a pool of resources? We need them when we cannot find the answers to what we are worrying about on our own. When we are overwhelmed with worry, we feel tense and confused and generally have a low mood. Sometimes, people feel inadequate when they cannot figure it out themselves, and that intensifies whatever they are worried about. But just because we are struggling with something does not mean we are lesser beings. All of our skills, insight, and strength are still in the picture. We simply need additional knowledge or a helping hand to get on track. A good way to start is to figure out the way you prefer to receive information or support.

How Do You Approach the Day—and Life Issues?

The following series of questions is one of my favorite methods to find out how people like to get help and guidance. Answer each question to get a better sense of what you need.

When are you most alert? Are you a morning, afternoon, or evening person?

Are you a person who likes groups, one-on-one support, or figuring things out on your own?

Do you prefer to work step by step and create a specific plan of action?

Do you like to sit and look at the big picture and then let the answers come to you?

Do you like to approach problems by gathering information first or by getting opinions and then creating a solution?

Do you like receiving information by doing your own research or by brainstorming within a group?

What methods in the past have helped you figure out answers (for example, therapy, physical exercise, writing, coaching, or meditation)?

How to Use This Information

What did you find out? Are you a morning or night person? Did it surprise you that you like to handle things on your own, or have you always known that? The reason this questionnaire is important is that you can now use all the information from it the next time you are worried. When you find yourself worried about something and need to figure out the best way to approach it, you can use the information from the preceding questionnaire and start working on it. So let's take a test run with what you discovered. Think about something that is worrying you at the present time, and let's apply the information you've learned.

Your Plan of Action

- Fill in this sentence: I am worried about (my next paycheck, my health, my daughter's grades, etc.)_____
_____.

- The best time of day for me to think about this issue is (consider your answer from the previous questionnaire and plan accordingly)_____
_____.

- I would like to figure out a solution by (consider your previous answers and decide whether you prefer to resolve stuff on your own, with a friend, with a group, etc.)_____
_____.

- In order to work on this issue, I want to (consider your previous answers and whether it makes sense to you to create a step-by-step plan or to focus on the big picture until a course of action or ideas comes to mind)_____
_____.

- In order to know whether this is a good solution, I want to (consider whether you prefer to gather information on your own or get some opinions)_____

  _____.

- If I plan to gather information, I will get it from_____

  _____.

- Going forward, I will take action to keep myself from worrying about this by (consider whether you would like to work with a coach, therapist, or spiritual counselor; exercise; write; etc.)_____

  _____.

So let's say you discovered that you function best in the morning and like group support and working step by step. If you are worried about something right now, you can apply that information to help you find solutions. Maybe you need to get up a little earlier, get some exercise in, sit down to think about your problem, and plan to meet with a few friends for some extra input after work or when the kids are napping. This is a "getting prepared" technique.

Throughout our lives we will have to contend with worrisome issues and problems. I know we can break free of the loop of worry. I have seen it happen hundreds of times in my therapy practice and workshops. I have witnessed the relief that people feel when they learn different ways to cope and get their bodies and minds working in harmony. From their experiences,

I have observed that the more we know, understand, and act on what is worrying us, the more we can provide for ourselves the support we need. When our bodies and minds are in sync, as opposed to being in conflict, it is easier to make clearer choices and decisions. Imagine being able to use that kind of knowledge to handle the sometimes overwhelming worries of life.

The more you can accept and understand who you are and how you function, the faster you will find support for your worries. Trusting your choices, experiences, and good sense will go a long way to keep you in balance. Identifying why you worry and what you are worried about is the next big step on the *Worried Sick* journey.

CHAPTER TWO

Recognizing Symptoms

In Chapter 1, we looked at how worry can and does affect our bodies, minds, and spirits. Now it is time to do more detective work and find out the degree to which worry is hanging out in your life and how it is affecting you. We will look at how the symptoms of worry can manifest physically, mentally, and spiritually—our three different tiers. As you look at these areas, try to remember that this is not about being judgmental but really about observation and understanding. I've had many people in my practice become self-critical once they see how they have been contributing to their worry. They judge themselves for overworking, overeating, or needing to be in super control. Yet most people turn to these ways of coping because they had to find a way to stay afloat while they were growing up. They did the best they could to take care of themselves in difficult situations. Now they can find a better way, and so can you; the more you recognize how you are handling worry in three key areas, the more you can make any necessary adjustments.

Effects of Worry

Physical Effects

The physical effects of worry often provide the best clues to how we are really being affected. The bodily symptoms that show up, both externally and internally, are powerful teachers about what we need to pay attention to.

Let's first look at the external factors. My observations of the body and how emotion is communicated focus on what is being expressed through the language of unconscious movement. *Unconscious movements* are all the little movements you make with your body when you are worried, such as tapping your feet, wiggling your ankles, or rolling your neck to relieve physical tension. Those movements are your body's nonverbal expression of what is going on inside you emotionally. Unconscious movements are the tiny motions we make without actually realizing we are making them. For example, you may bite your lip or clench your teeth when you are worried. You may crack your knuckles or bite your nails when you are stressed. What becomes important to notice is the link between that movement and what you are feeling and thinking. Sometimes those feelings are about that particular moment and what you are concerned about. Other times, it happens because we are carrying the weight of a long-held worry in our bodies. That old expression "carrying the weight of the world" comes to mind.

All the neck rolling, foot shaking, and finger tapping become clues to your worry. You are going to start becoming aware of these things so that you can use the information to help you. Now, we are not putting every gesture you make under a microscope. Can you imagine? You would not be able to take a step! No, we are only going to work on raising your awareness around some of your unconscious movement. For example, why do you bounce your leg up and down as you sit in your yearly review? What does it mean when you find yourself massaging your hands over and over after you visit your doctor? Could these gestures indicate that you are worried? Yes, they could. Once we make those connections, we can use the knowledge to create self-care. That is what occurred with one of my patients.

Peter came to see me because he was feeling blah in his life. Those were his words: "I just feel blah." A quiet man in his midthirties, Peter owned his own business and had been in a relationship for the past two years. He described himself as happy in his profession as a financial planner and was content in his personal life as well. He told me his girlfriend had expressed a desire to get married and that he was considering it. We talked about his blah feeling, and after I ruled out a diagnosis of depression, I continued to observe him from a body-mind perspective. One of my observations was that every time he spoke about getting married his foot would rapidly move up and down. He would describe his relationship with his girlfriend in generally good terms and tell me he was at the point where he thought he *should* be considering marriage. Each time he used the word *should* or words to that effect, his foot would start moving.

I decided to explore that foot motion with Peter and asked him if he was open to an observation. He said he was, so I reported to him the following: "I notice that whenever you talk about how it is time for you to get married, your foot starts going up and down. Are you aware of it?" He looked at me with surprise and said, "No, not at all." I said, "Would you like to explore the motion and see if it means anything?" Peter said he would, and we agreed that if either of us noticed his foot moving in future sessions, we would stop and explore what it might mean.

In a session soon after, Peter was discussing his girlfriend and their recent talk about a time frame for them to get married. Peter's girlfriend—soon to be his fiancée—wanted to plan for something in the next year, whereas Peter saw it happening in maybe two years. However, he had not shared his desire for a longer waiting period with his girlfriend and was basically agreeing with whatever she wanted to do. She, of course, had no idea that Peter saw things differently. As he talked about this, his foot started moving, but this time Peter picked up on it himself. "I see it," he said, "and I guess now is the time to find out what it means." He looked at me and said, "What do you think?" I smiled and replied, "First, what do *you* think, and more important, what are you feeling about getting married?"

Peter paused for a moment and said, "Well, I'm not sure I'm ready. I love my girlfriend, but I feel I want to wait a little bit longer. I'm worried that my finances are not where I would like them to be, and that makes me uneasy. I'd like a little more time to save up some more money and then go from there. I know my girlfriend might not be happy, and I can guarantee my parents won't be, but it feels too soon."

I asked Peter if why his foot was moving so much made sense to him. "Yeah, I'm nervous about this whole thing, and it's making me jumpy." Over a series of sessions, Peter and I talked more about his worry, and he finally was able to share his concerns with his girlfriend. She had no idea he felt this way. To Peter's surprise, she was understanding and supportive of his needs. They reached a plan that incorporated both of their needs, and Peter felt relieved. The power of tracking his unconscious foot movement gave Peter a voice for his worry.

How about you? Are you open to doing some checking yourself? If so, look at the following checklist. Remember, this is not an exercise to make yourself crazy by watching your every move but rather a way for you to uncover information about what may be worrying you. The main thing is to see whether you notice any body movement that is happening over and over again. Movements such as neck rolling, face rubbing, jaw cracking, and hand wringing are often expressions of worry. If it seems that you are doing quite a bit of those kinds of movement, you may have something else on your mind. Use the Body Talk Checklist as a way to discover what that something may be.

Body Talk Checklist

Think about when you started to notice any unconscious movement of your body.

- ❑ When did you first start noticing it?

- ❑ What type of movement do you observe yourself doing?

- ❑ When does it seem to happen?

- ❑ Are you with anyone or by yourself?

- ❑ Are you worried about that situation or person?

- ❑ What are you worried about?

- ❑ Describe how that issue makes you feel.

- ❑ Do you have any idea what you may need to help you feel less worried about this person or situation?

- ❑ Is there a way to provide all or any part of what you may need to feel more in charge?

If you are unable to come up with any solutions to what you may need to feel less worried at this time, this book contains many exercises and checklists to help you do so. As you go along, you will be able to choose the ones that are right for you.

When we explore our physicality, we include our physiology. Our physiology includes all the systems within our bodies that help us function. This means how our organs, tissues, muscles, and cells work together to keep us alive. So we are not just looking on the outside of our bodies but also the inside. The human body with all its intricate systems and functions has a lot to tell us when we are worried.

The physical signs of worry include the following:

Gastrointestinal distress (constipation, diarrhea, gas, and digestion problems)
Headaches
Skin problems (rashes, blotches, breakouts)
Shortness of breath
Hair loss
Teeth grinding
Nail biting
Jaw tension
Loss of appetite
Nervous eating
Increased heart rate
Muscle tension (neck, shoulders, lower and upper back)

I once had a patient who developed severe jaw pain as she was dealing with the terminal illness of her father. As we explored her jaw tension in therapy, she realized that she literally clamped down on her worried and sad feelings. She did not want to display them in front of her father and cause him any additional distress. She tried, understandably, to keep a brave face when she visited him. Yet when she allowed herself on different occasions to weep openly in my office about the emotional pain she was experiencing, her jaw tension would inevitably ease. Once this patient made the connection between her jaw and her worry, she began to notice when she became tense in that area. Eventually, because of the psychological insight on her situation and the emotional understanding of what she was holding back, she was able to share her concerns and worry with her father. What was remarkable was that her father, even though he was sick, wanted to be there for her, too. He reassured her that her expressing her feelings did not upset him but in fact allowed him to feel more connected to her. My patient's jaw pain was her personal signpost for both her unexpressed worry and her eventual healing.

I know that figuring out what symptoms belong to what problem can be confusing because they can be and are often associated with other medical conditions. Your detective work plays an important role and entails tracing the history of these symptoms. Later in the chapter I will show you how to apply your observations, such as when you noticed your physical symptoms occurring, and then see if they are connected to any worrisome event. From there you will add information such as when you noticed your body's reaction and what action you may need to take to feel better.

My colleague Kelly Brogan, M.D., confirmed that many physical symptoms can appear when we are worried and stressed: "In my experience, patients with chronic medical conditions often experience a pattern of exacerbation that is directly linked to their levels of psychological stress and pressure. Conversely, when subjective stressors are addressed and managed, physical symptoms (chronic pain and dermatologic, gastrointestinal, neurologic flares) may abate. To this end, identifying sources of stress and triggers for worry such as interpersonal conflict, job performance, and financial strain can be important for physical wellness. There is no doubt that stress, from ordinary to traumatic, translates into bodily manifestations."

I, too, have seen patients who have a certain medical condition that under normal circumstances is under control. However, when they are overloaded and under mental pressure, their condition worsens. Because I know them so well and understand the body-mind connection, it usually does not surprise me. I encourage them to find good medical support to alleviate any discomfort they are experiencing and try to help them work through whatever is triggering the upset, so that they can feel better.

Both Dr. Brogan and I have had patients who did not recognize the connection between their physical distress and their mental state. As a therapist who focuses on the body-mind connection, I can see why. Many people learn to disconnect from their bodies in order to handle painful emotions. They may experience that pain from either the inside or the outside. Perhaps they grew up in a violent household and had to numb themselves from the pain of either being on the receiving end of that violence or witnessing it. Maybe they were taught to be stoic or that life is tough, so they better "toughen up." Or it could be that they were neglected or criticized and started to feel bad about themselves. As their self-esteem plummeted, they had to find a way to distance themselves from all that internal strife, and they did so by spacing out or acting out. When we need to feel in control in horrible or stressful situations, we do the best we can, which sometimes means rejecting our bodies.

I have also found that many others are simply taught to dismiss their instinct and focus only on logic. Instinct, as I mentioned earlier, is our innate system of self-care. It is that part of you that hesitates before walking down a certain street because something does not feel right or causes you to pause before you enter a building because the person in the doorway sends off a weird vibe. If your instinct is telling you that your body has reached its limit in terms of physical and emotional health but you ignore it, you could end up with some unpleasant symptoms due to worry that might have been avoided. If we stop trusting our instinctive abilities, we lose touch with a primal way of understanding issues that may not be immediately apparent to our minds.

The more connected you are to your body, the more you can pick up on the information it is sending you. The first step is to become aware that your body is sending you a message; the next step is to listen to what it is saying. In my experience, once my patients become aware of the body-mind relationship, that awareness becomes a powerful tool. They can then exercise their options and choose how to manage their worry and keep themselves healthier. You, too, can develop that awareness.

Take a first step by reading over the following questions.

Do You Worry at the Expense of Your Health?

Grab a piece of paper and look at this list of questions. Without overthinking, just write down what first comes to mind.

1. How is your overall health these days?

2. Do you feel energized or tired?

3. Are you experiencing any physical problems such as bad digestion, skin issues, muscle aches, or headaches?

4. How long have these symptoms been happening: a day, a week, a month, or longer?

5. Are these unusual symptoms for you? If not, have they happened before? If yes, what were the circumstances?

6. What is different in your life now?

7. Is there any correlation between your physical symptoms and certain stressors in your life? If so, what might that connection be?

What did you discover? Are there events or people in your life that are causing you to worry? What did you notice about your physical symptoms? Sometimes it can surprise us that our upset stomach has nothing to do with what we ate but is more about what is eating us up inside. After you have your symptoms checked by your health practitioner, it can be illuminating to see if there is another cause. As we'll see, worry and its physical impact are something that you can observe and track. Once you know the source, you will then be able to think about what to do about the cause. Maybe it will be an obvious action, such as stating your feelings or asking for help. Or maybe it will be an action that is obvious only to you, such as taking a day off or getting exercise to relieve your stress. As with any healing process, awareness is the first step toward managing your health. Once you become aware, you can choose how to manage your physical reactions. Later in this chapter, I will give you some tools you can use to help yourself feel calmer.

Psychological Effects

We all have different levels of ability when it comes to handling worry. How worry affects our psychological health is unique to each of us. The psychological impact of worry is how our mental and emotional functioning becomes different when we find ourselves preoccupied with stressful events. The study of our ability to balance logic and emotion is the heart of psychology—the science of understanding our rational thought processes as well as the range of our emotional responses.

Most of us have a range of psychological responses to worry, and we develop a variety of coping mechanisms. A *coping mechanism* is a pattern of thinking or behavior that we create or adopt to handle problems. A coping mechanism can have a long history, such as always being accommodating at work because you were not allowed to speak up as a child; or it can be a more recent response to a stressful situation, such as coming in to work super early every day because you fear you will be fired. Unless you know that your position is being considered for downsizing, you are trying to feel more in control by coming in early. A coping mechanism may be created in response to an irrational, imagined circumstance or behavior that is in response to our current reality—a means of gaining control when we feel out of control.

Our psychological reactions to worry can range from mild to serious. The following are some minor psychological reactions to worry:

Feeling irritable
Feeling nervous
Feeling tearful
Feeling clingy

More serious symptoms can include the following:

Anxiety
Depression
Fear
Panic
Anger
Rage

All of these types of psychological consequences and their severity are important to investigate. However, I want to take a moment to address a bit further *when*, and *if,* the psychological response you are having seems to be more than just worry.

Even though depression and anxiety can happen when we are worried, they are also serious psychological states of the mind that are separate from what we may feel when we worry. People who have been diagnosed with depression and acute anxiety are not just excessive worriers. No, they suffer from real illnesses with organic, biological, and emotional roots that must be given proper attention. How can you tell the difference? The severity and longevity of the symptoms are clues to whether someone has either serious depression or anxiety. Each disorder has a set of criteria and symptoms, which need to be evaluated by a licensed mental-health professional. If you feel you have been suffering for too long with general feelings of either depression or anxiety, please get yourself the support you deserve. Many treatments are available for both of these conditions, and relief can be found. I have provided a general list of resources at the end of this book. In the meantime, look at the following to see if you are being psychologically affected by worry.

What Is Your Mind-Set These Days?

In order to find out how you react psychologically to worry, answer these questions. These are general questions and should not be used to gauge more serious psychological states of mind. Again, try to just go with the answers that come to you and not second-guess.

How would you describe your general state of mind or mind-set these days? Are you happy, sad, upbeat, calm, feeling blue? Write down what feeling first comes to mind.

Do you feel energized or tired?

Are you experiencing any physical problems such as bad digestion, skin issues, muscle aches, or headaches?

How long have these symptoms been happening: a day, week, a month, or longer?

Are these unusual symptoms for you? If not, have they happened before? If yes, what were the circumstances?

What is different in your life now?

Is there any event or series of events that may be affecting your mind-set?

How about work stress, personal or family health concerns, or the economy?

How long have you been feeling this way?

On a scale of one to ten—one being calm, ten being very upset—how would you rate your current emotional state of mind?

How is your current mind-set affecting your day-to-day life?

What did you discover? As you looked at these questions, did you notice a relationship between issues you are concerned about and your emotional state of mind? What number did you give yourself regarding your current state of mind? If it was high, was that a surprise? If you are feeling fine, great, but if not, bringing awareness to what is contributing to your unhappiness will help you feel more in control. Self-knowledge is a powerful tool and puts you in the driver's seat. You will be able to try some additional strategies as we go along to help you find clarity and peace of mind.

Behavioral Effects

Although we are going to address some specific behavioral components of excess worry in other chapters, we will take a broader look at some of them now. When we are affected by worry and perhaps even overwhelmed by it, chances are that our behavior is going to change. Some of those changes will occur because of the worry itself, and some will occur because of the choices we make to handle it. The distinction between the two is important, yet the root remains the same.

Worry affects our behavior in areas such as sleep, eating patterns, and the ability to concentrate or complete our daily activities. If we are affected by worry, these areas may be disrupted. We may struggle with falling asleep, find ourselves on a steady diet of sugar and caffeine, or fall behind in our work responsibilities. Over time, these disturbances start to take on a life of their own. The less sleep you get, the more your ability to concentrate and make clear decisions becomes compro-

Stress and Worry's Downward Spiral

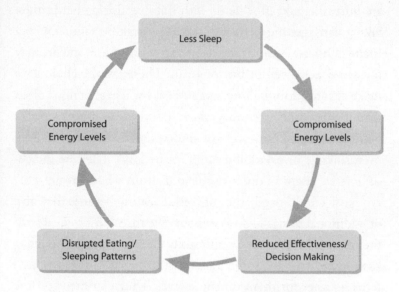

mised. The more your decision-making abilities are thrown off, the more your eating or drinking patterns may be affected. The more these patterns are disrupted, the harder it is to maintain your energy levels. The more your energy levels are affected, the more your physical and psychological health are affected. This is when you may find yourself becoming self-critical or anxious. You may find an old illness or injury flaring up. Then another set of behavior mechanisms comes into play, and they are the ones you use to handle these symptoms. Now I know why no one has ever said that worrying is easy.

We all have our individual strategies or coping mechanisms

that we use to handle worrisome situations. Some of them are nurturing and provide us with stability during hard times: taking naps, getting a massage, taking a walk, or talking with a friend. Others, even if they feel effective in the moment, may not serve us so well in the long run. These are the choices we make that are habitual but not so healthy. These actions often involve the words *over* and *under*. They are decisions such as over- or undereating, over- or underexercising, overspending, overdrinking, or overdoing drugs of any kind. They are the behaviors we adopt in order to shield us from what is really worrying us. Yet ultimately they are self-defeating because they give us additional things to worry about. We then have to deal with the consequences of those unhealthy choices. Oddly enough, I have found that for some patients, turning to unhealthy patterns is easier for them on some level. They can focus on the familiar complaints about their weight, debt, or money problems as the source and distract themselves from what is really worrying them.

Despite all of these reasons, I feel it is important to turn a friendly eye on why we are making these choices. We want to become aware of our coping mechanisms without condemnation. We need to make healthier, conscious choices that keep our best interests at heart, without berating ourselves for our actions. Negative self-talk tends not to be a good motivator when you are trying to change behavior; it usually has the exact opposite effect. Using compassion and self-awareness to shift old patterns will help you make permanent changes in your coping skills.

Is Worry Invading Your Life in the Guise of New or Changed Behavior?

Look at the following questions and consider whether your behavior is reflecting how affected you are by worry.

Aside from any ongoing medical issues, how is your overall health?

What do you notice about your day-to-day functioning?

Have there been any changes in your spending, eating, alcohol intake, and so on?

What sorts of changes have you noticed?

Have you found yourself using other substances to cope?

Are you experiencing any outbursts of emotion—crying more than usual, snapping at those around you, or generally being in a bad mood?

Do you find yourself wanting to withdraw?

Has anyone commented or given you feedback on your emotional state?

Has anyone commented on your drinking, eating, or spending?

Are you avoiding decisions or activities that require your participation?

What did you find out? As you answered the questions, did you discover any changes in your normal pattern of behavior?

If you are behaving differently, it is probably in response to something that feels overwhelming and difficult to handle. As I mentioned earlier, if you feel that these behavioral patterns are reflecting a more serious inability to cope, it is important and empowering to find good sources for medical and psychological help.

We have looked at three key ways that worry shows up in our lives. Understanding the importance of the physical, psychological, and behavioral ways that worry influences us provides us with a road map that we can use to interpret the signs of worry. I cannot emphasize enough how connecting to your body and mind will help you dismantle the confusion you feel when you are preoccupied and concerned. In my previous book, *Find Your Inner Voice: Using Instinct and Intuition Through the Body-Mind Connection*, waking up the body and understanding its signals was vital to accessing self-awareness and insight. The more you can learn to trust all the sensations, signals, and behaviors, even the destructive ones, from your body and mind, the better you can take charge of your life. It's like having insider information on how to address your worry. So how do you do it? How do you access that knowledge? Let's start the process.

Reduce Symptoms with a Worry Break

As you can see, worry finds ways to creep into our lives. We can feel tossed about by events happening both in and around us. Sometimes it is hard to keep our footing. As we have explored the three areas where worry can appear, we know that they are often intertwined. Yet the more we create a little time in our day to reduce excess worry, the more balanced we will feel. In a later chapter, we will look at some ways to untangle from worry's effect, but here are two quick worry busters for you to try now.

A good way to start working with your worry is to use your body as an ally so that you can notice the signals it gives you. Also, the more you can get comfortable and balanced in your body, the more you will be able to manage the symptoms of worry. The following two exercises will help you start creating a connection to your body and reducing your stress. You can do these at work or at home or both places. If you are at work and you have an office, shut the door and carve out ten minutes for yourself to do one or both of these exercises. If you don't have a door to close, you can certainly do this exercise with your eyes open, or pop into a conference room, or, if need be, a bathroom stall. If you are at home, find a spot where you can be alone; if that's impossible, you can keep your eyes open to watch your kids and still reap the benefits from the exercises.

Worry Buster 1: Take a Breather

Use this worry buster when you feel like you have a perpetual knot in your throat, are experiencing an increased heart rate, or are nervous.

1. Place your feet on the floor and see if you can feel the ground underneath your feet.

2. Close your eyes and let your hands rest comfortably in your lap. (You can do this with your eyes open, if necessary. Just focus them downward.)

3. Take a moment and notice how you are breathing.
Is it shallow or deep? Are you holding your breath in any way? Are you breathing all the way into your chest, stomach, and abdomen? If it feels like your breath stops at a certain point, see if you can breathe more deeply into that stuck place.

4. Now, inhale slowly and count to four.

5. Exhale slowly, counting to four.

6. Inhale slowly, again counting to four.

7. Slowly exhale for four counts.

8. Repeat three or four times, or more if needed.

9. Let your breathing return to normal.

10. Slowly open your eyes.

Just sit and see if you notice how your body and energy levels feel. Do not be concerned if you do not feel a difference right away. Sometimes it takes a few tries to connect with your body and start feeling more relaxed.

Worry Buster 2: Heat the Hands

Our next exercise helps move all of the mental energy that worry creates from your head to your hands. Whether you are actually feeling mental tension or it is imagined, the following exercise helps you shift your focus and relax. Note that this is especially good for headaches.

1. Place your feet on the floor or sit cross-legged.

2. Close your eyes and let your hands rest comfortably in your lap or on your knees, palms up.

3. Check on your breathing. As you inhale and exhale, notice whether you can allow your breath to go all the way into your chest, stomach, and belly.

4. Now place your attention on your hands and imagine them heating up.

5. You can picture your hands filled or surrounded by colors such as yellow and gold.

6. You can imagine that your hands are inside heated gloves made of a soft cloth.

7. You can picture your hands holding two gold or yellow balls. (If you have trouble picturing your hands, you can hold something in your hands and simply place your attention there. You could use rolled-up socks, two pieces of fruit, your glasses case and wallet, two mugs or cups, or anything that provides you with a little sense of weight.)

8. Focus on the heat, color, or weight in your hands for five or ten minutes.

9. Slowly open your eyes.

Start Your Worry Journal

Moving your state of mind away from worry and shifting your body from high alert is a great way to break the cycle of worry. Even if we cannot pinpoint the exact cause of the worry when we start, we usually find some clarity when we finish.

Meet Matt. From the outside, Matt appeared to be a man who was thriving in his business while balancing a happy home life. Though he was an accomplished businessman in his forties and seemingly healthy, he constantly worried about succeeding in his profession, securing financial security for his family, and maintaining his physical health. He was the kind of guy who would read the business section of the newspaper and scan it with eagle eyes in order to catch the slightest shift in the economy. He also frequently doubted that he worked enough hours to keep his company going or spent enough time exercising to ward off illness. He was constantly nervous and thought he was getting an ulcer. The nerves and the ulcer shouldn't have been his first clue that something was wrong, but for Matt they were. His body was sending out distress calls that he was too tense and worried.

Many people are chronic worriers like Matt; they have come to accept that feeling a little nervous or ill at ease is commonplace. But a feeling of low-grade nervousness, a general feeling of dissatisfaction, the sense that what you are doing is not making you feel better, and the inability to relax—whether at work or home—are commonplace only when you are holding on to a lot of worry and the stress that comes with it. I had

Matt start the whole process of understanding his worry by creating a worry journal for him. We did this so he could target the physical, psychological, and behavioral areas he needed to pay attention to. You, too, can go through these steps as I describe the methodology we used.

Tracking Your Worry Factors

To get started, I had Matt identify *when* his worrisome thoughts would first show up. This required him to notice when he started to worry and how his mood changed. If he did notice a change, he was to mark down the time of day. All I wanted him to do was raise his awareness. This would help move him from his general state of worry and narrow it down to a specific cause. The more Matt could pinpoint when he started to worry, the more he could trace the worry back to the original trigger. Triggers are the stimuli or reasons we shift from one state of mind or mood to another. If we note the things that trigger us, we can understand what we need to address or change.

Tracking Your Worry Signals

The next area Matt and I investigated was *how* he was being affected by his worry. That meant he had to start noticing whether his reaction to worrisome situations was physical, psychological, or behavioral. Identifying whether you are experiencing any changes in your day-to-day functioning will help move you away from feeling like you are a victim of worry. You can use this awareness to address what you may need to do to keep you from getting stuck. Again, this does not mean that what you are worrying about will disappear. What it will do is help reduce the amount of emotional energy you are expending on a particular problem. A great place to start is with the checklists that appear earlier in the chapter. Matt and I used many of the same checklists to help him as well.

If Matt noticed that his heart was pounding or his neck was tense, he used that information to note that this was a physical reaction. If he realized that he was feeling irritable or anxious, he was able to tell that he was being affected psychologically. When he found himself wanting to eat candy all day at the office, he used the information as a behavioral signpost. Excess sugar consumption meant that Matt was trying to handle whatever he was worried about by using food.

Matt was a bright man, and I wanted to appeal to his intelligence. I also wanted to help him learn to trust his emotional and physical responses. In order to do so, I had to help him get out of his head, so that things could make more sense. I know it sounds odd to move away from logic when you are trying to figure out the answer to a problem, but believe me, it works, and the move is only temporary. From my experience, including the body as part of any problem solving is highly effective. You have a powerful resource at hand when you understand that both the body and the mind respond to decisions that you have to make. If we can break up old, outdated ways of thinking by shifting our focus to something else, we allow for new insight. New insight facilitates and reinforces new behavior. When we are trying to dismantle excess worry, why not use all of our abilities?

Now it's your turn to start a worry journal. At first, it'll seem as though we are working backward because we are not focusing on the source of your worry right from the start. The reason for this is that sometimes we do not know what the triggers are for our worry, and we cannot connect to the things that are causing them. So we work backward. Looking at when and how the worrisome thoughts unfold will eventually lead us back to the cause.

As you will see, the worry journal is something you can copy right from this book. Keep the journal at your workplace or at home, and whenever you find yourself confused by something that is bothering you, you can jot down your observations in your journal or on your computer.

Before you begin writing in your journal, close your eyes and take a few deep breaths. Inhale slowly through your nose and exhale slowly through your mouth. Do this about four or five times, slowly inhaling and then exhaling. You can always take a worry break and use one of the worry busters to guide you toward a calmer you. After you have taken some good deep breaths, open your eyes and start working with your journal. Jot down all your observations as you go along.

Time of Worry

DAY/TIME

Think about when you started to feel worried, overwhelmed, or bothered.

When did you first notice it?

What day was it?

What time was it?

Can you remember what happened right before you started getting worried?

Describe what happened.

What was your reaction?

Worry Symptoms

Now you are going to focus on how the worry is affecting you. You will look at the three areas we discussed earlier in the chapter and notice whether you are responding in any of those ways.

PHYSICAL
What are the physical sensations or reactions you are having? Describe them (tense, jumpy, uptight, head pounding, upset stomach?).

PSYCHOLOGICAL
What thoughts and emotions are you experiencing? Use your own words. Are you anxious, nervous, cranky, irritated, sad, or weepy?

BEHAVIORAL
How are you handling things in your life? What behaviors are

you noticing? Are you overdrinking, working late, not sleeping, or eating poorly?

Worry Triggers

Use the information you observed about when and how your thoughts and mood shifted to see if you can pinpoint what the cause might be. These triggers can be personal or professional. They could be long-standing issues or something more immediate. Again, before you look at these questions, close your eyes and take a few deep breaths. Open your eyes when you are ready.

EVENT

Was the trigger event something in your personal or professional life?

Was this something that just happened, or is it an ongoing situation?

How did you respond (took action, did nothing, were caught off guard)?

When you think back on the event, what are you feeling? Are you sad, angry, confused, or concerned?

What do you think you would like to do about it (let it go, think about a plan, go for a walk, speak to a friend)?

When you imagine taking that action, how do you feel? Are you empowered, scared, out of control, or calm?

Is there anything you need to do before you take an action?

Here is an example of how the worry journal would look.

Situation	Day/Time	Trigger	Symptoms	Action	Future Action
Long line at the bank and I'm worried I'll be late to pick up kids	Mon., 2:00 P.M.	Only two tellers	Heart pounding Cranky	Did nothing	Ask for manager Call babysitter

If you need help figuring out what actions to take in response to your triggers, you can use the Three Cs approach to help you figure out what you need to do in order to let go of your worry.

The Three Cs

Calmness

What would help you release any physical tension you are experiencing in relation to your worry? Think about physical movement (either vigorous exercise or stretching of your muscles), meditation, slow deep breathing, neck massage, manicure, acupuncture, or chiropractic adjustment. Are there types of movement or body treatments that you are drawn to, that you really like? What are those treatments and forms of movement? Help your body and mind unwind by choosing physical activity and self-care therapies that relax you. Later in the book we will explore in more detail some ways for you to discover what your body responds to.

Clarity

How can you create the space you need to clear your head and find the answers you need? Is there a place in your home, office, or neighborhood that affords you some peace and quiet? Letting things settle down in your mind will allow you to find the kinds of information you need to address your worry. Also, what answers did you get from reviewing the checklists and questions in this chapter? Armed with knowledge, you can decide what you need to do to move from fear and paralysis into action. Action takes you from a place of helplessness to a place of empowerment. Remember to take periodic breaks from "breaking news." Too much information, all the time, can cloud your perspective.

Community

Think about the different sources you can turn to for clear, trustworthy advice during this time. Within your present community, whom could you contact for emotional, psychological, or spiritual support? Sometimes we just need to talk out our fears with others, either to find answers, to receive guidance, or just to be heard. What friends, loved ones, therapists, health practitioners, or spiritual advisers can you turn to for support right now? Where can you get the kind of information you need to help you feel more empowered and alive? Websites, bookstores, online communities, groups, and classes are available all the time. Think about what would help you feel better and see if you can find the resource to get it from.

The more you can control the things in your life, the more you will be able to manage the worries that occupy you today. Of course, if your symptoms of worry remain persistent, make sure you get medical and professional support to help you through. Now let us take a deeper look at how worry appears through our belief systems.

CHAPTER THREE

Understanding the Roots of Our Worries

I am pretty sure that if you had the choice between worrying or not, you would choose the second option. After all, who would purposely want to have worry as a constant part of their lives? Not too many people I know. But what if your tendency to worry were something so automatic and habitual that it kicked in even before you realized it was happening? Almost like a cat whose ears prick up the moment it hears the sound of the can opener and races into the kitchen to be fed. The fact that the can opener may have nothing to do with the cat does not even register. The cat is just automatically reacting to the sound that it has come to associate with food. That is the kind of response that ruled Matt's life with his continual worry about what could and might go wrong. He automatically worried without pausing to consider whether what he worried about was actually a reality—and most times for Matt, it was not. His reaction was similar to that of another patient of mine, Jennifer, whose chronic state of worry kept her from experiencing more joy.

Jennifer was a young artistic woman in her late twenties who felt that her life was an ongoing series of struggles. Though sensitive and articulate, Jennifer not only distrusted her creative abilities but shied away from romantic relationships. She often shared in therapy the worry and deep sadness she felt about the state of her life. Her original reasons for why she constantly worried were certainly valid and important issues to understand. Yet over time, it became apparent that Jennifer was stuck in a particular way of viewing her life. Each time something good happened, either a personal or professional achievement, she dismissed its validity. She brushed it off as not a big deal and went back to trying to convince me how bad things were for her. No matter how many times I pointed out the falseness of her thinking, Jennifer would not allow herself to be pleased with her accomplishments. She recognized that she was getting in her own way but felt frustrated by her inability to believe in herself.

Jennifer was not consciously trying to be miserable. On the contrary, she desperately wanted to be happier, but she just could not believe it was possible. Like Matt in the previous chapter, Jennifer had a hard time seeing her current life with a more balanced viewpoint. She tended to reject the facts that showed her that things were not so bad. This was a coping mechanism that she had developed over time, which now operated on autopilot.

Worry as a Defense

Whereas Jennifer's pattern was to dismiss good things and positive accomplishments as they occurred, our businessman Matt tended to worry in advance and on a continual basis. He described himself as a self-made man who had basically raised himself from childhood despite being surrounded by obvious luxury. He lived in a large home in a wealthy section of town, and his parents were well known in the community. But the inside picture did not match the outside. Matt told me he was lonely as a child because he was often left by his parents with an older sibling for long periods of time as they socialized for his father's business. Because of this, Matt learned to become self-sufficient, handling many adult responsibilities at an early age because his sister, who was ten years older, was understandably not interested in being a parent all the time. He also described to me that when he was six, he made his own breakfast daily and got himself to the bus stop for school because his father left for work very early and his mother did not like to get up until much later in the day. Though his family did not lack for money, it was not given freely even for basic things such as school supplies and clothes. Matt's father often questioned Matt's requests for money and gave only the absolute minimum and nothing extra. Matt quickly learned that he was going to have to make do on his own. He delivered papers from the time he was ten, worked at a restaurant while he was in college, and eventually got a business degree by going to school part time in the evening. After college he met his wife and they had two lovely daughters. Through hard work and dedication to his education, Matt accomplished many of the things he had set out to do. Yet he tended to overwork and do more than was necessary at his job. He found it hard to delegate some of the tasks that could easily be handed off to his staff. He just could not seem to allow them to help. He felt that no one could handle the responsibilities as well as he could, and yet he tended to worry over many of his decisions.

This spilled into his family life as well. Even though he provided more than enough financially for his wife and two daughters, he constantly worried he was falling short. He ruminated over his daughters' futures and wanted to shield them from many of the hardships he had experienced. This was one of the reasons he originally sought therapy. He realized he was not enjoying the life he had worked so hard to create. When I asked him why, he said, "I never take anything for granted." And by not taking anything for granted, Matt was in a constant state of worry.

When Matt and I started exploring his need to stay on top of all things all the time, we discovered he had some long-held perceptions about his right to happiness. He could not relax into the success of his accomplishments because he truly thought that security was an illusion. Matt believed that any accomplishment had to be guarded over vigilantly or it would be taken away. This mirrored the way he felt it was when he was a child. He received inconsistent parenting, and any security he had within his family felt fleeting. Sometimes his parents were there and sometimes not. Matt developed a way to cope with this inconsistency. He just never let himself enjoy the moments in his life when things were going well. Instead he worried that those moments could be taken away, just as he did when he was a boy. So he worked extra hard and stayed vigilant so that he wouldn't have to rely on anyone or anything. For Matt, overworking and worrying about his life was his way of staying secure by fending off any imaginary disasters in the future. But what it mainly did was keep him from being present and living the life he was in now. Matt was stuck in time, held there by an outdated image of himself as a boy.

Worry as a Belief System

Jennifer also did not arrive at her tendency toward chronic worry out of the blue. She had developed some deep-seated beliefs that stemmed from her childhood. While growing up, Jennifer had witnessed her parents arguing incessantly. Their fighting usually involved physical and emotional violence but only toward each other. They constantly attacked each other's abilities, attractiveness, and intelligence. Many times Jennifer hid in her room until the storm of fighting between her parents had passed. Even then, it was hard for her to relax and trust that everything was okay. She knew that eventually the temporary harmony between her parents would fall apart and they would soon begin battling again. She kept waiting for the other shoe to drop. From this abusive pattern of her parents, Jennifer learned to believe that good feelings were only temporary and there was no use believing otherwise.

Because of her chaotic background, Jennifer felt that if anything, even the smallest thing, went wrong, it was proof that her life was a failure. She could not comprehend the idea that good things, including personal and professional accomplishments, could be sustained. How could she? All the evidence from her past pointed to the fact that no matter how happy her parents seemed to be in the brief moments when they made up, they would eventually start fighting again. She internalized, which is to say she started saying to herself, the same hurtful things her parents said to each other and found it easy to doubt her abilities, attractiveness, and intelligence. Jennifer's unhappy childhood caused her to cultivate the negative core belief that she could not trust herself or others to be happy.

Core beliefs are long-held beliefs about ourselves and the world around us that we learn early in life. These beliefs can be either positive or negative. They generally influence the way we view our abilities and lead our lives. If we feel good about ourselves, we tend to feel that way about the world around us. If we feel bad about ourselves, we tend to be uncomfortable in the world at large. The kinds of beliefs that are intertwined with worry are often negative core beliefs, long-held negative opinions that are either formed over time or caused by a single event.

Negative core beliefs are typically formed from the verbal and nonverbal messages we received growing up from our parents or caregivers. Both Matt and Jennifer formed belief systems from what they witnessed in their families. When not enough positive messages are given to counteract any negative messages, a distorted belief system is created. Of course, the belief system is faulty, and the person's perception is usually not in alignment with their current reality. But it feels very real to the person who has created it. If those feelings are not resolved or understood, then that person gets stuck in the past.

Negative beliefs also develop from having experienced a trauma, such as a serious accident, or a series of traumas, such as the constant fighting that Jennifer observed between her parents. Most people feel powerless when they experience trauma and can end up with a set of ongoing symptoms, worry being one of them. Other symptoms of trauma are anxiety and depression along with physical reactions such as headaches, stomachaches, and shaking. When your sense of security has been threatened, you tend to worry excessively about your safety and your ability to face and handle problems in life.

Even if you did not have a particularly troublesome childhood or adolescence, you can form negative core beliefs by absorbing the steady stream of unrealistic images from the media. For example, if you feel that you do not look like the ads you see or are not living the life that advertisers are selling, you can end up with a negative core belief about your own worthiness. This may cause you to worry about your appeal to others, or you may end up doubting your abilities. Whatever the source that created the negative belief, the result is that those affected are left feeling "less than" and helpless about their ability to change their view of themselves.

When you do not receive enough supportive feedback to counteract whatever negative messages have come your way, you tend to develop the distorted belief system I mentioned. This is caused by a lack of positive mirroring in your life. *Positive mirroring* occurs when someone else affirms and validates your positive qualities. If no one tells you that your parents' destructive behavior has nothing to do with you, you end up creating your own reasons for why it is happening. And because, as a child, you do not have the same ability to process thoughts and emotions the way an adult would, you end up formulating explanations that are inaccurate. Most times, children and teenagers blame themselves for the problems their parents are having or are experiencing. They have to find a way for their world to make sense, so they come up with their own answers.

The same goes for unrealistic media images. As we visually take in what we *should* look like as opposed to what we *do* look like, we end up with contrasting viewpoints. We compare our ability with that of celebrities, other famous people, or successful businesspeople. A celebrity's ability to look a certain way appears ideal and effortless. A wealthy business owner seems to radiate assurance and unwavering confidence. Even as we mature, we contend with how we should age and what success we should be achieving through a very specific media lens. Some of us start measuring ourselves against a scale that gets tougher and tougher to match. We find ourselves striving toward a false standard of perfection and worrying that we are not making the grade.

These public standards plus the messages created from our upbringing form an environment for self-critical thoughts to grow. Unless something or someone else offers a different perspective, these thoughts stick. These beliefs are formed from false evidence and do not reflect the truth of who we are. Yet for the child who created and absorbed them in an environment that reinforces them, they feel very real. Ultimately, these convictions are carried into adulthood and become part of our identity. Consequently, without any real understanding or working through of why those critical thoughts formed in the first place, you can end up stuck with an outdated and unrealistic view of yourself. What is one of the ultimate impacts of all of these on you? You end up endlessly comparing yourself to your image and wonder why you don't feel competent or content.

When chronic worry and negative thinking start to emerge as a pattern in our lives, it is usually because outside events or stress are causing us to feel the same way we did when we were younger. In other words, a conflict at work or a struggle with money can make you feel the same way you did when a similar conflict occurred when you were a child. You end up experiencing the same feelings you did back then, and one of the ways you try to gain control of the situation is by using the same behaviors. Eventually, as we talked about in Chapter 1, that state of stress can wreak havoc on both our bodies and our minds. Unfortunately, it can also have a big impact on our personal and professional happiness.

One of the reasons negative core beliefs have a large impact on us is because they are so deeply ingrained. They do not respond well to logic, and they cause us to worry. They have a stubborn quality to them, and even though you may know that your perceptions do not make sense, it is hard to let them go. A good way to tell the difference between a negative core belief and a momentary insecurity is by how you respond to reality. I know that sounds funny because most of us feel we respond very well to reality, but I am really talking about how you respond to feedback. Distinguishing whether you have a chronic negative mind-set or are just hitting a brief mental roadblock is important to clarify. A great way to figure this out is to gauge how easily you can shift your outlook from worry to one that is more positive.

If you were having a brief moment of self-doubt, your viewpoint would end up shifting as soon as someone pointed out the truth of the situation. When we allow ourselves to take in the facts of a situation and our frame of mind shifts, it usually means we were just feeling insecure and needed reassurance. For example, suppose you gave a presentation at a meeting, and afterward you said to a work buddy that you did not think you did well. Your colleague responds by saying, "Are you kidding? Everyone was talking about how well you did and that you seemed so confident!" If you were able to take in your pal's perspective and feel your viewpoint change, you were just having temporary feelings of worry. You would not continue to ruminate over what had just occurred. You would accept that you had given a good presentation at the meeting because you got positive verbal feedback. The same would apply to other areas of your life. You would believe that your children are thriving because they are healthy and happy. You would trust that you are fit because you had a positive doctor visit. All the evidence presented to you would illuminate the truth of each situation, and you would typically feel calmer.

However, if you still felt bad about your presentation, your children, or your health, regardless of the feedback, you have probably run into a chronic negative belief. With these kinds of beliefs, your viewpoint would not shift so easily. An example of this would be if you automatically rejected a compliment or dismissed someone's positive feedback because you simply could not fathom their viewpoint. That is the kind of resistance I mentioned, which is a persistent emotional and psychological wall that does not allow your perspective to budge. Even if someone gives you facts and statistics to show that your observations are not accurate, it doesn't make a difference.

With negative core beliefs, it is hard to let go of worry and trust someone else's perspective. The positive feedback or reality of the situation does not affect your view. Like Matt, you may unconsciously be holding yourself to an unrealistic standard. You tend to go back to worrying about your life and what *may* happen because of your past experiences. It may be hard to believe, but the worry offers an odd comfort by providing something that is familiar and something you can control. As a patient once said to me, "At least when I am being negative, I am the one in charge. No one else can hurt me because I've already done it to myself." She was not the only one who felt that way.

Worry and Situational Negative Thinking

Not all of us fall into the category of chronic negative thinkers. We may not have the mind-set that causes us to worry excessively, but we occasionally feel vulnerable to situational negative thinking. *Situational negative thinking* occurs when a trigger from our current life causes us to worry or think badly about ourselves. The worry is triggered by a current situation and not necessarily by past negative core beliefs. A person experiencing this feels the same feelings as a chronic negative thinker, but the thoughts are not constant and are more fluid. People who suffer from situational negative thinking usually end up feeling unimportant for a short period of time in the face of present-day circumstance. These situations are triggered by a specific current event, such as having a fight with your spouse, missing a meeting because you overslept, or even falling off a healthy eating plan.

The result of this is that you end up temporarily feeling doubtful or insecure about yourself and your abilities. For example, perhaps growing up you struggled with school, and because of this you were teased by others for not being smart. Along the way you might have developed a harsh image of yourself and your value as a person. You may have developed some negative core beliefs because of those critical remarks. Those beliefs could have been thoughts like "I am dumb" or "Nobody likes me because I'm stupid."

Over time, as you conquered your academic problems, you probably let go of those old critical remarks. However, if in your current life your ability to complete a work project stalls or you receive constructive criticism from your boss, your old feelings of self-doubt may temporarily return. Again, they are created by a current situation that throws you back to a previous mind-set. Most times, if you get a good reality check along with some reassurance, that old way of thinking goes away. That is how you can tell the difference between the two types of negative thinking. Either way, whether it is chronic or situational, you can shift the causes of negative thinking when you track and focus on getting a more realistic outlook.

At times, all of us can shift our negative thinking to positive, and that is an empowering place to be. However, making that shift is not always immediately possible, and it is important to respect where you are in regard to worry and negative thinking. Most people do not want to hold on to negative beliefs about themselves, yet, as you saw, those thoughts can be triggered without warning. If we could always shift our thoughts by simply thinking positively, most of us would. Because there are times that we cannot, we have to approach the problem in a more compassionate and creative way. We are now going to look at a specific tool that I used with my patient Jennifer. Using this method is how we started to change things for her.

Worry's Hidden Message

Jennifer needed to find ways to stop worrying excessively and start trusting her perceptions again. She needed to find some tactics so that she could sustain artistic success and create loving personal relationships. This involved both working with her fixed negative beliefs and also challenging the foundation on which they were built. Investigating why Jennifer's worry was so constant, and then exploring the hidden message beneath it, would help her understand her unhappiness. This is an important concept to grasp. When we can start to look at worry as a messenger, one that arrives to give us emotional and psychological information, we can then start to move away from feeling stuck. Sometimes the only way we make changes is for things to become intolerable. We may not like the form in which our worry shows up, but if we use our energy to address the reason it is here rather than get caught up in it, we will feel empowered.

With Jennifer it was important to reassure her that the reasons her beliefs were originally formed were valid but now outdated. They were not serving her anymore. The initial purpose for having them was no longer needed, and they were now interfering in her life. However, advising her to just "think positively" whenever she felt negative could have ended up making her feel worse. Jennifer did not feel good about who she was on a deep level, so trying to persuade her to feel positively about herself was not going to work. Although nothing is wrong with thinking positively, there is no "one size fits all" solution.

Despite the current popular trend, telling someone to think more positively without understanding the complexity of what they are worrying about can often backfire. In fact, in the May 2009 issue of *Psychological Science*, researchers found that positive thinking did not improve mood; they reported that "positive self-statements can be ineffective or even harmful." They noted that this was true for people who had low self-esteem, which held true for Jennifer. In other words, if you do not have a long-standing good opinion of yourself, it is going to be harder to believe a positive statement. The other way positive thinking can be harmful is when you ask someone to focus on the positive things in their life when there may not be any. I found this out in a poignant session I once had with a patient.

My patient, a young woman in her early thirties, came into my office one day and said that she was feeling terrible. I asked her what she meant and she told me that everywhere she went, articles and books were telling her to focus on the positive and acknowledge the good things in her life. When I asked her what was so upsetting about this, she said, "How can I feel positive when I have so many bad things that are happening in my life?" I asked her to tell me all the bad things she was experiencing. She did and when she was finished, she looked at me and said, "What do you think? Aren't those horrible?" I looked at her and saw the pain in her eyes. I sat for a moment, took a breath, and said, "Yes, you have some horrible things happening in your life." Her eyes widened and she said, "You think so?" "Yes," I said firmly, "I do." At that moment, her eyes filled with tears and she started to sob deeply. Of course, I had a moment of insecurity because I could not tell at that point how my words had affected her other than by the fact that she was crying. After crying very hard for a period of time, she looked at me and said, "I can't believe you said that. No one has ever believed me before." She started to cry again, but the quality of her sobs sounded different from sadness. Later on, when we talked it through, she told me she had cried from relief. From an early age, her parents had taught her to be strong and often dismissed her feelings of upset and fear. Having me acknowledge the reality of her life validated her emotional reality. She shared that it did not make her feel like a victim to have the truth told—in fact, the exact opposite. After that session, she was able to start opening up to her strengths and the fact that she was facing all her difficulties with great courage.

For the record, I do believe in being both positive and realistic. I do think there are times when positive statements help keep us going, especially when they are authentic and we truly believe the words. I also know the importance of allowing ourselves to have deep feelings in regard to very real and painful situations. There are times for grief, anger, and deep despair, and that is part of being human. Having those deep feelings does not take away from our ability to find our emotional equilibrium again; in fact, it actually helps us. When we release and express our feelings, it is very cleansing to our psyche and gives us relief. When we are no longer burdened with emotions, we can often find clarity.

I have also found that when we have resolved enough of the root causes of why we doubt ourselves, positive, affirming statements can be wonderfully motivating. Until that process occurs, a blend of reality checking and action can help break up old patterns of thinking. When you fully understand why your perceptions are distorted, you will be able to let go of your worry and negative beliefs. Once my patient Jennifer realized she was not a bad person for creating a distorted belief system, she was willing to try to dismantle it. Let's look at how you can break the patterns of worry and negative thinking.

Breaking the Worry Pattern

Two practical strategies can help you when you find yourself caught in excess worry and negative thinking. The questions to ask are (1) "Do I need a reality check?" and (2) "Is immediate action the best solution?" Sometimes you will find that you need to address both questions. After you have explored these questions, it is good to determine whether your negative thinking is situational (triggered by a current event) or chronic (the usual way you view yourself and life). When the worry and negative thinking is situational, either strategy can be effective. When the worry and negative thinking is chronic, taking immediate action is generally the better choice. As we have seen, reality checking does not work particularly well for chronic negative thinking because the beliefs are deeply ingrained. By moving into action, the mind has to shift. It is hard to hold on to negative thinking when you are being forced to place your attention on something else, even if it is for a short while.

If you find yourself worrying about irrational things, try to figure out what has triggered this mind-set. Is this your usual view of things, or has it sprung up out of the blue? I am sure you already have a good understanding of how you operate in the world, but if you are unclear you can use many of the questions in the previous chapter, which help you explore what triggered your thoughts, to help you arrive at an answer.

If you discovered that your worry and the negative thinking is situational, you can give yourself or ask for a reality check. Using this strategy, you positively reframe any negative beliefs you are having by drawing on your experience of who you are as evidence. You think about the event and contrast it to how you have handled things in the past. You reflect back to yourself all of your erroneous thinking, which helps dismantle your current distorted self-image. You can also ask someone you trust to give you a reality check as well. Developing a more realistic perspective helps you understand that one moment of insecurity or indulgence does not define who you are as a whole. Here is an example of how this works.

Worry and Reality Checking

Sheila, a mother of two in her midthirties, was very much into healthy exercise and eating. She worked out on a regular basis and tried to eat foods that she felt were good for her. However, she did worry sometimes that if she did not exercise regularly, all her hard work would disappear. Sheila used to have a weight problem and had made a great effort to lose the weight and get fit. She had worked very hard on both her internal and external images of herself and felt pretty successful about the healthy lifestyle she had created.

Yet during a particularly busy month at work, Sheila came to see me and shared that she was feeling down on herself. Her job had required her to travel quite a bit, and it was harder for her to keep up her healthy routines. Sheila had found herself missing a few workouts and eating more junk food than she would normally like to. She told me she was feeling discouraged and feared that all her efforts to be healthy were disappearing. She worried that she was now on a slippery slope to gaining her weight back and was feeling scared.

This did not make sense to me when I heard it. Prior to this, Sheila had been very consistent in her workouts and how she handled her food intake. Yet now she was in my office expressing a negative belief about herself and her abilities. Sheila felt she was bound to regain her weight because, according to her, "I obviously have no willpower." If she did, she felt she would have found a way to keep her exercise and eating habits on track. I remember thinking that Sheila was very hard on herself and that we were definitely bumping up against an old negative core belief. The belief that she was out of control had been triggered by her inability to balance an unusually busy work schedule with her normal routines.

One of the first steps that I took with Sheila (and that you can do for yourself) was to acknowledge the feelings she was having, regardless of the distortion. This is important because despite the exaggerated perspective, which can happen to any of us at one time or another, it probably feels very real. After you have allowed some room to express your feelings, you can move on to a series of evidence-based questions. You are going to help your mind break free of the self-criticism by presenting the facts. For instance, with Sheila, who felt she had no willpower anymore, I said something like, "I get that you feel you have no willpower, but if that is the case, can you tell me who has been showing up for all those exercise classes you take?" I wanted to help Sheila remember all her past efforts and confront the part of her that was not in reality. My question caused her to slow down and think about the evidence. In this instance, she could not deny her dedication to her health and was able to shift her perspective. You can as well. Although it sometimes may seem easier to negate the truth or come up with reasons for why you need to worry, it will be difficult to hold on to those distorted beliefs once you have a chance to look at facts. Later in the chapter, I will show you a quick way to stay more in the present moment.

Worry and Taking Action

Taking action is another great way to shift negative thinking and worry. This is the tactic I used with Jennifer to help her move away from her chronic worry. David Burns, M.D., in his book *Feeling Good*, discussed how to get beyond depression coupled with procrastination. He wrote, "You have to prime the pump. Then you will get motivated, and the fluids will flow spontaneously" (Burns, 1980). In other words, sometimes the only way we can get focused on something other than our negative thoughts is to take action. This could mean moving your body, teaching yourself a new skill that is not overly demanding but requires focus, or writing down everything you have accomplished up to that point that you are proud of. As you move, exercise, chat with a friend, or write down your thoughts, you will be forced to shift your attention away from whatever is bothering you. Although those thoughts may not disappear completely, you will find that your mind has to adjust to the action you have taken. This gives you the opportunity for clarity and helps you break away from worry's hold.

Your choice of taking action provides you with a focus and diverts your attention away from the loop of worrying. The more you try taking different actions, the more you will observe what actually works. You will start to notice how you respond to the different activities you are trying, and then you can use that knowledge to guide you in the future. If you discover that the particular activity you chose frustrates you, choose something different. We do not want the action you take to compound the feeling of worry!

I had Jennifer try different activities to keep her from getting stuck in her chronic worry. We made a list of all the things she liked doing, such as singing, painting, and dancing. Whenever she found herself in a chronic state of worry, she made a conscious effort to take an action. She discovered that music and dance really helped her frame of mind. From then on, whenever she was stuck in her worry, she put on music or took a dance class. She made sure that the class did not require a dance background but was really for nondancers to just have fun. By taking action and continuing to explore her negative beliefs in therapy, Jennifer started to change. She became more optimistic as she realized she was in charge of her life now, not the ghost of her parents' relationship.

As you become more aware of the link between worry and your negative beliefs, you will be able to choose what to do in order to break free from them. From a body-mind perspective, you will experience how your energy changes as your thinking changes and vice versa. You start to become more aware of how your body feels less burdened, your thinking becomes clearer, and your mood lifts. You will enjoy the satisfaction of decoding the message tucked into your worry and how you use the knowledge to take charge. Here is an exercise to help you do so.

Worry Chart

You can use this chart in combination with the questions from the worry journal in Chapter 2 or on its own. Whenever you find yourself feeling worried and negative toward yourself, grab a piece of paper. Now, take a pen or pencil and make five separate columns or headings. Here are the headings for each column:

Worry Trigger

I Feel Negative and Worried Because

Is This a New or Old Feeling?

What Would My Best Friend Say?

What Action Do I Need/Want to Take?

Underneath each heading, you will jot down your thoughts and observations. Let's use Sheila as an example:

Worry Trigger	I Feel Negative and Worried Because	Is This a New or Old Feeling?	What Would My Best Friend Say?	What Action Do I Need/ Want to Take?
Fell off healthy eating and exercise routine because of travel.	I used to be overweight and fear I am back to the old image of myself.	I am basing this feeling on an old belief about myself.	"Sheila, you are fine. You will get back on track because you have the willingness and discipline to have lost the weight in the first place. You have worked hard and have the experience to know what to do."	Go back to exercising again and take a class that I really love. Choose a physical activity that makes my heart sing.

As discussed earlier, the more you track your worry, the more you will begin to know whether the negative thinking that it causes is temporary/situational or chronic/persistent. If you do not find relief from your negative thinking and it is causing you concern, be sure to support your self-care by seeking professional guidance. Again, resources are listed at the end of the book for you to use if you need them.

The Three Cs

Calmness

When you imagine moving your body so that you can stop your negative thinking and relax, what comes to mind? Think about the kinds of exercise or activities that would allow your body to let go. What kind of movement would help you tap into feeling good during and after? Do you feel you need to run, dance, walk, do yoga, do tai chi, do martial arts, or swim? Which physical activity do you know would create a sense of relaxation after you were finished? Tap into your past experiences, and if you are not someone who moves regularly, see what it would be like to take a walk, stretch, or move to music. Let your body help you let go of worry and negative thinking.

Clarity

Now that you have identified the type of negative thinking you are doing, what can you learn from it? Is there old, unfinished emotional business from the past that requires resolution? Are there changes that need to happen in your current life to help you feel more in balance? What can you take from what you have discovered and apply in your life now? Think about all of the experiences you have gone through from the past that required you to keep going. Use those experiences to validate your strengths and depth of character. We do not evolve as people without going through both good times and bad. Give yourself credit for your accomplishments large and small.

Community

Who is that person you can get a reality check from? When you imagine someone giving you a more realistic view of yourself and your efforts, who comes to mind? Is it a work friend, best friend, spiritual friend, or mentor? Is it a loved one, significant other, teacher, or therapist? Really think about all the different people in your life and whom you can turn to. Contemplate the variety of support you have and what each person's strengths are. Do you need a pep talk, someone to strategize with, a shoulder to cry on, or a more experienced elder? Once you decide what you need, choose the people you know who can fulfill that need to the best of their ability.

In the past three chapters we have been looking at all of the ways that worry gets created. From the past to the present, we saw how worrisome thoughts and feelings form. We can see how powerful our thoughts become over time and how important it is to disrupt their control. When we remember that we have the ability to change the path of our thoughts and feelings, we become more in command of our lives. Now it is time to look at how we can start unwinding even more of worry's grip and use the power of the body, mind, and spirit.

Part 2

CHAPTER FOUR

Unwind Your Mind

My friend Lisa started a brand-new relationship a few years ago and was feeling very optimistic about the new person in her life. As she and her boyfriend got to know each other, Lisa felt very strongly that this man could possibly be someone in her life for a long time. She was excited and happy for the first six months, and then she began to worry about the longevity of her relationship. As we met over coffee one day, Lisa asked me, "What if he breaks my heart? What if he is not who he says he is? What if I let myself really fall in love, and it doesn't work out?" I could only reflect back to her what she was asking me because I did not have any answers to her questions. "Okay," I said, "what if everything you are worried about comes true: He breaks your heart, he turns out to be a phony, you fall in love and it doesn't work out. What *would* happen to you?" Lisa sat for a minute and then said emphatically, "Well, I wouldn't like it!" "Yeah," I said, "I get that pretty strongly, but what would happen to you?" She stared at me, took a big sigh, and said grudgingly, "I *guess* I would survive." She spoke with such reluctance and exaggeration that we both laughed out loud. Even though her tone of voice was sullen, Lisa's conviction was pretty strong. She knew she would survive because she had a wealth of life experiences to remind her of her strength.

When we are worried, our minds can become a maze of anxiety and vivid imaginings. We speculate on situations in which we cannot possibly know the outcome. If we do know the odds, we often get caught up in a loop of fear. Sometimes, like Lisa, we become convinced that the worst will happen. We become locked into those beliefs. Other times we start with one worry and end up worrying about a whole lot more. We have a fight with our boyfriend or girlfriend and worry that they will break up with us, then worry what will happen when they do and if we will ever find another relationship. We might get an e-mail saying that our manager wants to see us regarding a project and worry that we will get fired and then worry how we will pay the mortgage and whether we will have to move in with our parents. If we do not do something to shift our perspective, we end up viewing the world and our problems through a very distorted lens.

This chapter is about breaking free from the hamster wheel of worry. We will be looking at a variety of techniques and exercises that will help you unwind your mind from worry. The focus will be on how to break the thought patterns and feelings that trap you in worry. You will be given different approaches for reducing your worry, and you can then choose the ones that match your needs. Because we all respond to worry in our own way, we most likely will have different responses to the methods that can help us. Some people find relief by relaxing their body, others by using logic, and others still by working with their spirit. I believe that all of the methods are helpful, and you will discover the ones that work best for you.

Using Logic to Move Beyond Your Worries

Many times when I am working with a patient, they describe a situation that they are worried about. As they lay out the details of their concern, I find myself listening for a couple of things. First, I listen for what I call the "incomplete picture." The *incomplete picture* involves the situation my patient is describing, what they feel about it, and where they may be stuck in their process. The person usually cannot see beyond a point because they run into a certain amount of fear. This fear prevents them from seeing a more complete picture with possible options from which to choose. Whatever the level of fear they are experiencing, it keeps them feeling stuck and they lose their ability to see a resolution. They worry about the unknown because their fear has kept them from exploring what they may need to feel better. In those circumstances, my job is to provide emotional support and ask a series of questions that hopefully will help them find the insight they are looking for. My questions usually involve trying to make the unknown more knowable. I also try to help my patients find ways to handle what they are worried about. The incomplete picture is completed when the person understands what they are feeling, faces their fear, and realizes that they have the inner resources to find answers. For example, once someone understands why they have been so afraid to ask for a raise, they can then start to take small steps toward preparing themselves to do so. Moving the fear or anxiety from the unknown to the known is like realizing the monsters under the bed are really just dust bunnies. Once you realize what they are, you can move forward again.

The second thing I listen for is something called *globalizing*. Globalizing occurs when we take one issue that we are worried about and expand it so that it encompasses our whole worldview. We may start out worrying about money, which moves to worrying about losing our home, our parents' home, our future children's homes, and so forth. Globalizing makes us worry not only about a single, current issue, but many things beyond the actual moment. When someone is globalizing, pointing it out will usually stop the worry from becoming a runaway train. If that does not stop globalization, I ask my patient to put all the issues beyond their control on the shelf for the moment and to focus on the one that first concerned them. Most times, once the original problem has been resolved, the person no longer feels worried about the other issues. This is a good technique to use with a trusted friend or loved one, whether you are the one listening or the one sharing.

Whether you find yourself struggling with an incomplete

picture or are globalizing a situation in your life, applying the logic of your mind is a great way to dismantle your worry. So, how do we go about doing that? I find that using the powers of observation, asking straightforward questions, and reminding ourselves of our strengths will help us arrive at answers. The more we can challenge the illogical hold of worry, the better we are able to let it go. In order to do this, we start with our own incomplete picture. We then identify what we are worried about and distill the fear down to the worst possible scenario. From there, we create a plan of action that will support us or resolve the issue. This exercise in logic will remind us that if we can create a plan that responds to most extreme situations, we can certainly make one when things are less severe. Here is an example of how to do it.

Logic Exercise 1: Completing the Incomplete Picture

Identify what you are worried about.

Is it a person, situation, or event?

I am worried because _____.

I fear that _____
- will happen to this person.
- will occur in this situation.
- will happen before this event.

Are you globalizing? If so, just focus on one worry at a time for now.

If the worst outcome occurs, what would that be?

Then what would happen?

After that, what would happen?

Then what? (Keep asking this question until you get to where you have reached the worst possible outcome.)

You are now faced with the worst-case scenario and need to make decisions.

What would you need to recover from this circumstance?

Where or from whom could you get help?

Is there anything you need to prepare for or do now that would offer you peace of mind for the future?

What would that be?

Now think about your original worry. What can you do to make the situation better?

If you are feeling dissatisfied with your current life and are worried about your future, the next exercise has you picture what you would need to feel more fulfilled and content.

Logic Exercise 2: Picturing a Less Worrisome Future

If my life or any area of my life were operating in the way I wanted, what would that look like?

How would I notice that my life was different?

What tangible, concrete things would I see that had changed (living space, people I spend time with, creative projects, career choices)?

How would it feel in my body to have things shift?

If there were one thing I could do to support a different way of doing things, what would that be?

Using Your Life Experience

When we are worried, it is hard to recall the times when we have persevered. I know you have probably had many episodes in your life when you came through difficult times with flying colors. I am sure there were times when you simply had to hang in there for your family, your significant other, a friend, or yourself. If we remind ourselves that we have had the inner strength and mental ability to figure out solutions in the past, we build confidence in how we will handle things in the present. Take a moment now to reflect on some of your past successes.

Self-Reflection Exercise

Think about some of the tough situations you have been through in the past.

Think about what allowed you to get through those times.

What were they (faith, stubbornness, strength, planning, community, mentors)?

Picture everything that contributed to the successful outcome of those circumstances.

Remind yourself that you took the steps and have the ability to do it again if necessary.

Letting It All Go Through Meditation

One of the oldest methods of reducing worry, especially when our mind is in turmoil, is the use of meditation. For many years, meditation has been used in the workplace but packaged as a "stress reduction" technique. The breathing and focus of meditation did indeed reduce stress, but the word *meditation* was unfamiliar to many in Western societies. Now doctors such as Andrew Weil, M.D., and Mehmet Oz, M.D., tout the benefits of meditation in areas of health such as blood pressure, mood, and chronic pain. Their endorsement comes from the research done in many different sectors about the benefits of meditation. For example, Colin Allen's 2003 article in *Psychology Today* reported that Jon Kabat-Zinn, Ph.D., conducted research on a group of stressed-out employees at a tech firm. Dr. Kabat-Zinn is a professor of medicine and founding director of the Stress Reduction Clinic and the Center for Mindfulness in Medicine, Health Care, and Society at the University of Massachusetts

Medical School. In his research, he recorded the brain waves of two groups of employees, those who had learned and practiced meditation for eight weeks and those who had not. Dr. Kabat-Zinn conducted brain-wave scans three times a week, both during the eight-week study period and four months later. The research team found a "profound shift in activity to the front left lobe of the brain." Those who meditated were calmer and happier and also ended up with better immune function than the control group.

This is one of many studies that show how meditation calms the mind and the body. Meditation is a process in which we allow our mind to settle down by consciously helping it relax through awareness. There are many different forms of meditation, and one of the simplest is placing your attention on your breathing, your heart, or a word. Some people meditate in silence; others use sound by repeating a word or phrase. Some people use guided meditation, which is following someone else's voice, while others use walking meditation, which combines walking with a focus on how your body is moving. As with all of the techniques and exercises we have looked at in this book, if you choose to try meditation, the form you select will be individual. You can experiment by learning meditation in a class, from a book, or by listening to a recording.

I asked my dear friend Amy Torres, who is an interfaith minister, spiritual teacher, counselor, and Heart Rhythm Meditation instructor based in New York City, to share her experience with meditation. Amy teaches a form of meditation called Heart Rhythm Meditation (HRM) that links the breath to the heartbeat, which she finds particularly effective. When I asked her why, she said, "The heart is our signature rhythm, just like our fingerprint is uniquely ours. Our hearts are our personal drums. When we synchronize our breath with our heartbeat, our entire organism, our physical system, enters a state of harmony, like an orchestra that is in tune." I liked her description, as it was definitely a reminder of the importance of connecting to our bodies. As we continued to explore this form of meditation, I asked Amy about HRM's impact on worry. She said, "Most of us try to ignore our heart when we are worried or stressed because it becomes arrhythmic, or races, or pounds in our chest. HRM helps us befriend our heart and use it as a steady anchor to ground us, help us regain our center, our composure. We learn to enter into a relationship with our heart, to trust its strength and power to work with us, not against us."

I know that many of us have had that feeling in which our heart is racing and we feel like we cannot catch our breath. Knowing that we can slow down our heart rate and calm our breath is reassuring. Amy describes how you know HRM is working: "On a physiological level, people will know it's working because they will experience a slower heart rate, lower blood pressure, decreased stress hormones, improved digestion, and better sleep. HRM also increases the body's ability to handle stress by increasing *heart rate variability*, which helps improve the immune response, increasing heart efficiency and the vital capacity of the lungs, which improves circulation and oxygenation of all tissues."

If you decide to explore meditation or the more modernly named *stress reduction technique*, you most likely run into our ever-chattering minds. That is exactly the point. With meditation, the more you can consciously learn to release and observe how our minds operate, the more relaxed you will feel. This form of worry reduction will, over time, provide you with a greater sense of clarity and ability to be present in your own life. I have included two meditation techniques. The first is the HRM technique provided by Amy, and the second is a breathing meditation that I have used. They provide you with a sense of the variety of meditation styles.

Heart Rhythm Meditation

Sit comfortably in a chair with your back supported.

Place your feet parallel and flat on the floor. Make sure your knees are even with your hips, and place the palms of your hands on your thighs.

Lengthen up your spine from your tailbone through your neck.

Relax your shoulders and let your head float lightly at the top of your spine.

Breathe through your nose.

Begin with an exhale and draw your belly button in toward your spine, so that it feels like a balloon that has lost air.

Allow an inhale to occur naturally and inflate your belly on inhalation. Invite the inhale to move up through your rib cage, expanding your lungs like an accordion.

Do this a few times, and after you are comfortable with this breath, pay attention to your heartbeat. You may be able to feel it as you breathe. If not, place your hand over your heart. If you don't feel it this way, take your pulse.

If you still don't feel it, don't worry, it's there. Just sense your heartbeat and link it to your breath by counting while you exhale, then while you inhale.

See which is longer and try to even out the inhale and exhale counting; for instance, 1 . . . 2 . . . 3 . . . 4 . . . 5 . . . 6 in and 1 . . . 2 . . . 3 . . . 4 . . . 5 . . . 6 out, connecting each count with your heartbeat.

This synchronizes the breath with the heart, and the results are relaxed concentration, stillness with alertness, and a grounded vitality.

Breathing Meditation

Close your eyes and sit in a comfortable position. You can sit straight up with your feet on the floor or with your legs up and crossed.

Place your hands on your knees, palms up.

Starting at 50 and counting backward, inhale on the odd numbers and exhale on the even numbers.

So, exhale at 50 to start, then slowly inhale through your nose on 49 and exhale slowly through your mouth on 48. inhale slowly through your nose on 47 and then exhale slowly through your mouth on 46.

Continue to do this until you reach 20. Starting with 19, inhale through your nose and exhale through your mouth on each number. So, inhale on 19 and then exhale on 19. inhale on 18 and then exhale on 18. Keep doing this until you reach 1 and then open your eyes.

Meditation definitely requires practice, and at the beginning, you may find it hard to stay focused. If you look at meditation as a process, one that requires you to let go of the idea of instant gratification, you will find it easier. There are many books for beginners, and it really is a matter of choosing the style that appeals to you. If you try either of the meditation techniques described here, don't worry if you lose your concentration. If you do, just bring your attention back to whenever you thought you were when your got distracted and start from there. Bringing your attention back to the moment is the discipline and process of meditation.

Boosting Your Concentration for Meditation

If you are looking for a way to enhance your concentration so that you can better meditate, then consider attempting games and puzzles that challenge your attention span. Incidentally, these same brainteasers are fun worry blockers all on their own—when you're focusing on completing a crossword puzzle, it's impossible for you to obsess about whatever has been troubling you. The other great thing about these types of games is that they are portable and can be done anywhere—at the office, at home, while traveling, or during your daily commute. You can even download them to your phone or computer, find them in your newspaper, or find books that offer hours of brain exercises in the form of entertainment. Consider trying out one of the following fun worry blockers:

Crossword puzzles
Word jumbles
Word finds
Sudoku
Solitaire (computer version or old-fashioned playing cards)
Computer games that increase memory and brain power

Negative-Thought Blockers

When you just cannot get your mind to slow down, the following exercises serve as excellent thought blockers and bring your mind into sync with your body. You may find that it is a challenge to coordinate your tapping and breathing, and you will relish the peaceful feeling that you'll find once you complete this exercise.

Breathing and Tapping Therapy Exercise

Sit comfortably in a chair with your feet on the floor.

Close your eyes and rest your palms on each knee.

Slowly inhale through your nose and exhale through your mouth.

Alternate tapping each of your knees, with your right hand on your right knee and your left hand on your left knee. Simply tap each knee by going back and forth; tap the right knee, then the left knee, and repeat the process for about thirty seconds at a steady pace. (It is just like when you are listening to music and let your hands keep the beat by tapping on your thighs or legs.) While you are doing the tapping, just keep breathing easily in and out.

Stop tapping and slowly take a deep breath in through your nose and exhale slowly through your mouth. Notice how your body and energy feel.

Repeat the tapping sequence three or four times or more if needed.

When you are finished, slowly open your eyes.

Chest-Tapping Therapy Exercise

Sit comfortably in a chair or on the couch, with your feet on the floor.

Close your eyes and place all your fingertips on your chest, between your armpits and sternum.

Tap lightly up and down on your chest, alternating hands.

As you tap, you can move your hands to the center of your chest and then back out to your armpits.

Tap on any area that feels tender, tense, or sore.

Continue tapping for about thirty seconds to one minute.

Let your hands drop to your lap and open your eyes.

See if you notice any difference in your energy or mind-set.

By the way, I often do this when I am watching TV and need to feel more relaxed. You can also do it sitting at your computer, before an important meeting, waiting in the car to pick up your children, or just when you need to feel more relaxed.

Worry and Our Five Senses

We have looked at how to use our minds when dealing with worry, and now we are going to tap into the power of our mind that controls our senses. Using our five senses—smell, taste, touch, sight, and hearing—is a terrific way to start unwinding our mind from worry. Because we already have this built-in system, exploring which of your senses responds best is a good place to start. Once you have decided which of your senses is the strongest, you can use that sense to help you disconnect from your worry. If you are not sure which of your senses is the strongest for you, try the following exercise. Just read through each description and then close your eyes. Notice how your body reacts and then move on to the next one. This is a great exercise to help you connect to your senses and bring them to life.

Identifying Your Strongest Sense

Take a few moments to sit quietly with your hands in your lap.

Think about your five senses. To which of these do you think you respond the strongest? Is it taste?

Does receiving or giving touch make you feel a certain way?

Do certain sounds evoke a physical reaction?

What about what you see or smell? Chances are, you rely on one of your senses more than the others. In order to discover which, choose one, try this exercise, and pay attention to your responses.

TASTE

Picture the most delicious, satisfying taste you can imagine—freshly baked biscuits, ripe blueberries, hearty chili, a favorite dessert, homemade lemonade, or whatever appeals to you the most. Imagine yourself taking the first taste and savoring the flavor as it rolls over your tongue. As you visualize yourself enjoying the flavor and texture of your favorite food or beverage, focus on how strongly you respond to your sense of taste. Does your mouth water? Do you find yourself sighing with pleasure or relaxing from the imagined warmth of a particular food or drink?

TOUCH

Think about the most relaxing, stimulating, or otherwise pleasurable touch you can ever remember feeling—the softest cashmere gliding against your skin, the warm hands of your significant other, a comforting hug, a luxurious bath, holding your child in your arms. As you imagine yourself enjoying the texture, the security, and the softness of touch, pay attention to how your body feels. Focus on the physical sensations and how you respond to your sense of touch. Do your shoulders feel less tense, your neck looser, or your face less tight?

SOUND

Imagine the sounds that make your energy level rise or fall, like a piece of music that energizes or calms you. Perhaps a sound that really resonates with you is the crashing of ocean waves, the tinkle of wind chimes, the rustling of leaves, or the contented purr of your cat as she naps on your lap. Maybe it is the laughter of your child or the sound of a train blowing its whistle in the distance. Really focus on the sound you chose, imagining it as if you were hearing it right at this moment. How does your body respond?

SIGHT

Picture the sights that make you feel peaceful, joyful, and serene—a night sky dotted with thousands of stars, snowflakes falling and dusting the trees, the smile of a significant other. Imagine the vivid colors of a summer sunset or the yellow stalks of wheat in a farmer's field. Focus on your body as you see this world before you and notice how your body feels when you take it all in. Do you feel warmth in your chest, sense your stomach calming down, or notice your breathing deepen?

SMELL

Think about scents that make you feel happy, content, calm, or energized: a spicy cologne or delicate perfume, the tantalizing smell of cookies baking, a fresh bouquet of your favorite flowers, leaves burning in a bonfire. Imagine yourself experiencing an aroma that brings you pleasure, slows you down, or wakes you up. Notice how strongly any of these scents affects your energy. Do you feel more alert and awake or relaxed and sleepy?

Disconnecting from Worry Through the Senses

Now that you have determined which sense is your most dominant one, look at the following suggestions by experts to find the best way for you to unwind your mind and body. Choose the ones that appeal to you or modify them so that they are effective and uniquely yours.

Taste

We will explore in detail in a later chapter the power that food has to help us with worry. For now, though, think of the different tastes and textures of food that help us feel calmer or give us sustaining energy. This could be a warm beverage like cocoa in the morning to start our day with a smile, or an herbal tea at night such as chamomile, peppermint, or orange spice to soothe our spirits. Perhaps you can make a crunchy salad filled with carrots, crisp lettuce, and fresh cucumbers to chomp out excess tension. Sometimes for comfort you will want your favorite pudding, soup, or mashed potatoes. I bet many of you have your own special concoctions that appeal to your taste buds alone. So whether you prefer an energy-packed smoothie filled with berries and protein powder on a summer morning or a bowl of clam chowder on a rainy afternoon, your sense of taste can help you feel better. For a more complete list of foods that can help you remain healthy and balanced when you are worried, go to the end of Chapter 6.

A CALMING EFFECT

I want to mention another worry reliever, and I'm putting it here because you normally take it orally. This particular suggestion is great for when you need to alleviate your worry, fear, and stress, because it's quick and easy. It's called Rescue Remedy and it's from a line of flower essences called Bach Flower Remedies, which are found in your health-food store or online. Bach Flower Remedies are used for a variety of emotional conditions and were created by Dr. Edward Bach. Rescue Remedy is made up of five different flower essences and is the most popular of all the flower remedies because of its calming effect. Rescue Remedy comes in a bottle with a dropper and is in a 50 percent water and 50 percent brandy base. You put the drops right into your mouth, under your tongue, or in a glass of water. You can also get Rescue Remedy in a non-alcohol formula, spray form, or in pastilles, which are chewable tablets. Each form of Rescue Remedy has instructions for you to follow, and you can go to the Bach Flower website at www.rescueremedy.com or your local health-food store to find out more information. Rescue Remedy also comes in cream form; you can use it on your hands, body, and face as a speedy way to achieve calmness.

Touch

Leigh Hansen is a licensed massage therapist and the founder of Remedy Massage Therapy, located in New York City. She works with a variety of clients and also specializes in pregnancy massage. She offered the following information about muscle tension and the healing properties of touch. "Our muscles react to worry by guarding, tensing, and shortening, which are all stabilizing measures. They are the body's way of battening down the hatches and fortifying itself against the anxious messages the brain is sending. Unfortunately, short, tense muscles tend to stick together and restrict movement. The less muscles move, the less oxygen and nutrients are circulated throughout the body. Fatigue and toxins build up, and pain is often a result."

I asked Leigh how touch could help with worry, and she said, "Using touch to release muscular tension allows emotions that need to be let go of to come to the surface more easily. After a massage, clients are more relaxed and yet focused. Usually they can connect to what some of their stress has been about and become aware of how their bodies have been managing the stress through different places of muscle tension." I picture what Leigh described as literally letting the worries flow out of you as your muscles are encouraged to relax through the touch of a massage.

In addition to massage therapy, there are many other ways to ease worry through touch. Acupuncture, reflexology, therapeutic touch, and reiki are all techniques that use energy to heal. You can also ask for a hug, rub your favorite lotion on areas of tension, get a pedicure or manicure, or try the following self-comforting exercise.

Butterfly Hug

Find a comfortable place to sit.

Close your eyes and take a couple of slow, deep inhales and exhales.

Cross your arms so that your right hand is resting on your left shoulder or upper arm and your left hand is resting on your right shoulder or upper arm.

Give yourself a hug or squeeze and take a deep breath and then exhale. Let your hands gently pat the tops of your shoulders or upper arms. You can also rub the tops of your shoulders or upper arms. As you do this, you can continue breathing in through the nose and out through the mouth in a slow, easy manner.

Try doing the butterfly hug for about five minutes or until you feel calmer. Then open your eyes and let your arms drop down.

Sit for a few moments and observe how your body feels.

Facial Massage

Hold your hands together with your palms touching and your fingers pointed away from your chest.

Rub your hands together back and forth for a few minutes, as if you are warming them up on a cold day or holding them over a campfire.

Close your eyes and move your hands up to your face. Place your fingers over your eyes and rest your palms on your cheeks. Gently make outward circles with your hands, letting your fingers and palms move lightly over your face.

With your eyes closed, use your fingertips to make small inward and outward circles all over your forehead, temples, eyes, cheeks, mouth, chin, and jawline.

Let your hands drop to your lap and open your eyes. Notice how your face and overall energy feels.

Sound

In my previous book, *Find Your Inner Voice*, I had readers tap into the power that making sounds has on the human body's energy. Letting out the emotional expression that is held inside is a terrific way to raise your spirits. However, here we are going to explore how *listening* to sound eases your worry. Most of us have a favorite piece of music that we listen to or sing to when we are feeling certain emotions. My friend and colleague Jane Burbank is a licensed psychotherapist, voice teacher, and singer in New York City who specializes in integrating music and other nonverbal body-mind techniques with traditional talk therapy. Jane has witnessed and worked with the power of sound with many of her patients and students. I asked her to describe her experiences and make some suggestions for using sound. Jane shared these thoughts: "A way an individual can self-soothe is to play 'new age' (nonprogrammed) music at home and to move to the music in any way that is comfortable. Nonprogrammed music allows the person to get out of their head and not think about 'what comes next' in the musical pattern. I tell people to just focus on and experience the way their body feels as they listen to the music." When I asked Jane what impact doing this would have on worry, she explained, "The experience of 'interacting' with the music through the body is very centering and gets people out of their heads and into their own experience in the moment." She went on to say, "The effect of playing/hearing/feeling the sounds and holding the instrument moves us from an overly cognitive focus. This shift from overthinking, which normally causes spiraling anxious thoughts, what-ifs, worry, and out-of-control/ out-of-body experiences, brings the individual's experience into the body and emotions, allowing a person to be inside themselves and thus reducing worry."

The cognitive focus that Jane is talking about is the kind of mind-heavy thinking we get into when we are worried. So the next time you are worried and need to give your mind a break, put on your favorite piece of music and trust that you will know quickly if it is helping you feel better. Remember, sometimes we need calming music to relieve worry, and at other times we need to turn it up full blast to discharge all the tension we are feeling. I also believe that nonmusical sounds are soothing as well. Those sounds can be the purring of your cat, the waves breaking on the shore, or the wind blowing through the trees. If you cannot find those sounds close to you, you can always buy recordings of them and listen to them when you want. Here are some activities that Jane suggested for using sound, both to make sound and to listen to it.

JOIN A LOCAL CHOIR
Singing encourages correct and effective breathing. Making music with your own internal body instrument and being surrounded by others making music is supportive and stress relieving. This is an easy, fun thing to do if you make the time commitment, which can vary with each choir or singing group.

PURCHASE EASY-TO-USE INSTRUMENTS

Drums, chimes, singing bowls, and the like can be played without having to have a musical background. People can buy, at little cost, any of these instruments and play them briefly at home to self-soothe through body/emotion experience.

Sight

When I was growing up, my father would build fires in our fireplace, and after he got them burning brightly, he would say with satisfaction, "Now that's a roaring fire." My brothers and I would sit and stare into the flames for what seemed like hours. Patients of mine have talked about watching the orange colors of the desert sky or looking out over the wide expanse of the Grand Canyon. Friends have shared how they have been lulled into calmness by the ever-changing surface of the ocean. Beautiful paintings and serene colors seem to slow the turbulence in our mind. Many people I have met have shared with me how using what they look at eases their minds.

What vistas are you drawn to? As you remember and contemplate the scenery and images that bring you peace, what comes to mind? When you are feeling worried, you can literally go to those places or find paintings, colors, or places in nature that are similar in feeling. If you are urban bound like I am, try the following quick exercise:

Sights for Sore Eyes

Find a comfortable spot to sit and rest your hands in your lap.

Now close your eyes and imagine something or somewhere that makes you feel calm, peaceful, or inspired.

What floats up to your mind?

Is it a serene lake, a beautiful skyline, a vivid painting, or soaring mountains?

See if you can focus on all the details that you remember from that image.

Notice all the colors and shapes of what you are looking at.

Take a deep inhale and exhale. Do this about three or four times.

Open your eyes and notice how your energy and body feels.

Take yourself to a movie, a museum, or your favorite park. Immerse yourself in the different sights of your community. You can try a technique I call "camera ready." Take your camera or cell phone and focus on capturing a series of pictures around a specific theme such as dogs, cool architecture, fountains, flowers, kids, or colors. Look for those images and take a bunch of pictures. Afterward, sit down and review them, noticing how you feel as you do so. This technique helps you shift your mind-set because as you are looking for specific images, you also bring creativity and energy into your life.

I also believe there is nothing like a good movie either at the theater or in your home to help shift your mood when you are worried. Getting involved with a good comedy, adventure, or mystery takes your mind from the present and allows you to have a real break from your thoughts. I do think what you choose to watch is important to consider. When you are worried or stressed, it is not a good time to get involved with a violent or tragic story line. I tell my patients to be very discerning about what they watch when they are feeling low. Let's take a moment to remind ourselves of our favorite films. What are your favorite movie comedies? When you think about those films, how do you feel? What are your favorite action or adventure films? What do you notice about your energy as you think about those types of films? What are your favorite mystery or suspense movies? How do those films engage your imagination? Do you have a favorite romance film? When you think about the plot, how do you feel?

Knowing what you like to watch and how it affects your worry is a great asset. The next time you are feeling worried and want a real or "reel" break, let yourself get lost in a film.

Smell

Are you are a person who responds to different soothing smells? Then using aromatherapy and essential oils may be a good choice. Aromatherapy is an ancient healing art in which essential oils are used to support the body's natural ability to realign and heal. Tara Keegan, a certified clinical aromatherapist, explains how the scents of essential oils work on the human body: "An essential oil is the life force or essence of the plant from which it was derived and is what makes the plant unique. The oil is considered 'essential' because without it, the plant could not live. The distilled extracts from plants—essential oils—may be found in any portion of the bush, flower, or tree and give each oil its characteristic aroma, chemical makeup, and healing properties." She goes on to say, "The scent of essential oils can affect the body in a variety of ways. Aromas can be sedating, invigorating, oxygenating, and healing. The fragrance of the oil travels by way of the olfactory nerve pathways directly to the limbic system in the central portion of the brain where emotions are stored." Basically, when we smell the scents of essential oils, the part of our brain that processes emotions is affected.

So if you discovered from the earlier exercise that you respond strongly with your sense of smell, using an essential oil would be a good choice. Tara recommends the following oils for relaxation and to reduce worry.

LAVENDER OIL
Lavender is a universal oil that has been known to balance the body and mind. This oil is excellent to use for calming and balancing. Lavender oil can be dabbed or sprayed on the wrists, temples, heart, or area of concern.

LEMON OIL
Lemon oil has been used to lower blood pressure, reduce anxiety, gain clarity, and promote a sense of well-being. You can

dab the oil on areas of concern such as the temples, chest area, wrists, or neck. Avoid exposure to direct sunlight for three to six hours after use.

PEACE AND CALMING OIL

Peace and calming oil is an essential oil blend of tangerine, orange, ylang-ylang, patchouli, and blue tansy. This combination of oils has been used to help reduce anxiety, stress, and tension. These oils also promote relaxation and help with sleep. Diffuse the oil by placing some drops on your hands and then apply under your nose, on the back of your neck, and on the bottoms of your feet, or drip directly into your bathwater. Avoid exposure to direct sunlight for three to six hours after use.

Remember, these oils are recommendations and could be a great way for you to use scent to reduce worry. You may already have your favorites and use them. If you find yourself drawn to other scents, fragrances, or oils, by all means trust your instinct and use those as well.

The Three Cs

Calmness

We have taken a look at using our minds, bodies, and spirits to lift the effects of worry. As you read the different techniques and try the ones that appeal to you, remember that you are looking for the best ways to feel calm. Calmness will have a specific meaning to each of you, but the overall feeling is that you are at ease in your body. Your breathing and heart rate will feel relaxed, and you will not feel agitated or tense. Trust that your body will let you know when you have reached this place. Exploring the different mind and body techniques in this chapter will help you achieve this.

Clarity

Whether we reach clarity by using logic, by using our five senses, or through stress reduction and meditation, knowing that we can find a way to do so brings peace of mind. In this chapter we have explored approaching the incomplete picture and globalizing. We have looked at a variety of ways to gain clarity about what is worrying you. Whenever you have an issue that is troubling you, it is important to clear out the agitation and upset that is clouding your perspective. Once you have done so, you can create a plan of action.

Community

As you have seen, many resources for support are out there. Whether your worries are large or small, physical or emotional, you can find people and places to help. Some approaches will be more mainstream, whereas others have a holistic feel. You will be the judge on what techniques address your worry the best, and feeling better will be your best gauge. Research, read, and ask for information that will alleviate your concerns, and consider what would appeal to your dominant sense. Perhaps a cooking class would offer the right atmosphere to a person whose dominant sense is taste; a live concert at a local club, theater, or school would be a great environment for a person whose strongest sense is sound. There are as many health practitioners as there are techniques. Trust your friends, colleagues, and instinct to find the right ones for you.

Going forward, we will begin looking at some of the different areas where you can find relief for your worry. A good foundation of self-care is important for us to feel solid and steady as we handle life's difficulties. Look over the following chapters and see if one or more of them jumps out at you. If so, take the time you need to go over the information and provide for yourself the support you are looking for.

CHAPTER FIVE

Move Your Body

If you engage in any kind of physical activity, you probably do so because it provides you with a sense of well-being, you want to stay healthy, or perhaps both together. Movement also benefits your mind and can have a big impact on worry. Whether you take a walk every morning with a friend, hit the gym for boxing after work, or follow your favorite yoga DVD in the afternoon, moving your body will move your mind. So many times I have had the experience of having my own mind cluttered with thoughts and concerns before I exercise. Afterward, I find I have more clarity and focus.

This chapter looks at the importance of physical movement and how it can shift us to a place where we feel more relaxed and clearheaded. We will look at why moving the human body provides such a direct means of relieving worry and raise your awareness of what your body may be expressing through how you want to move it.

In this chapter, we will investigate different ways to move and have you choose the right type of exercise or movement for you. If you are looking to reduce your response to worry, learning what type of movement makes you feel happier and calmer will be very important. After all, if you associate exercise with drudgery, you probably will not continue. I know so many people who choose exercise based on what they think they should do as opposed to what really makes them feel good. When you do something you enjoy, you tend to keep doing it. Even if you have never exercised before, trying something you *think* you may enjoy will help you take the next steps forward. Along the way, both a fitness expert and a psychotherapy colleague of mine will provide additional information and techniques on how to approach movement for optimal stress and worry reduction. They will share from their experience of working with clients and patients who come into their offices in one state of mind—worried—and leave in another.

Moving Away from Worry

I do not know about you, but at this point in my life I only participate in exercise that I really like. I try to choose activities that match my mood, and I allow myself to change to other things when I get restless. This does not mean that every time I take a particular class or do a workout, I am 100 percent enthusiastic. I wish that were the case. For the most part, though, I do like doing some kind of physical activity because even if I have to talk myself out the door to get to the gym or park, I usually feel better afterward.

Exercise as a Stress Reliever

There are known medical reasons why exercise helps us feel better. Our heart rate goes up, which positively affects our metabolism and energy. We breathe more deeply, and that allows more oxygen into our lungs. Getting more air gives us energy and helps us feel more relaxed. In fact, I think learning how to breathe more deeply is a great step toward getting your body to move. The breathing exercises we looked at in Chapter 2 are good ways to reconnect and slow down your breathing. Although breathing exercises contribute to the same good feelings that moving your body does, they are not the only reason why we feel better and more focused.

We all have probably experienced similar things when we are moving. People talk about the runner's high or the deep feeling of relaxation and clarity they feel after a yoga class. I have had patients tell me of psychological insights that occurred while they were exercising. Many speak of the physical release that we have been discussing that brings about calmness in the body or the clearness of thinking that occurs because the body has released tension. No matter how you get there, moving your body helps you relieve worry.

Consider the following exercises when you want to relieve stress and pent-up energy:

Tennis or racquetball
Bicycling or a spinning class
Kickboxing

Belly, zumba, or hip-hop dance
Running or jogging
Jumping rope

Movement as a Distraction

In studies at British Columbia and Northwestern universities, one of the ways people reach moments of insight has been a topic of great interest and research. In a *Wall Street Journal* article, Robert Lee Hotz wrote about how we get to the "aha" moments in life. *Aha moments* are those times when we achieve insight but do not appear to be actively thinking about the problem. Kalina Christoff, a cognitive neuroscientist from the University of British Columbia, was quoted in the article: "People assumed that when your mind wandered it was empty." However, she went on to say that measurements of brain activity showed that "mind wandering is a much more active state than we ever imagined, much more active than during reasoning with a complex problem."

I found this research interesting as it relates to movement and exercise. Even though when we are exercising, we do not appear to be actively focused on a problem, in reality our brains continue to sort things out. Have you had that happen? I know I have. I will be trying to sort out a problem and then head to the gym or go for a walk. While I'm moving my body, I will start to figure out what I need to do. Even though I think I am doing a very different activity, my mind is on the job. This ability of our multitasking brain has been studied and monitored. In the *Wall Street Journal* article I just mentioned, psychologist John Kounios at Drexel University in Philadelphia and his colleague Mark Jung-Beeman at Northwestern University wrote that they "used brain scanners and EEG sensors to study insights taking form below the surface of self-awareness." They studied volunteers working on word puzzles and found that the ones who seemingly reached solutions out of nowhere were not simply guessing. They found that that their subjects' brains bustled with energy and broadcasted "that signal one-third of a second before a volunteer experienced their conscious moment of insight—an eternity at the speed of thought." Their brains showed all this activity even though the volunteers were not exactly in sync. The word-puzzle answers they were looking for hit their conscious minds a tiny bit later.

I also think that movement provides another kind of mental support. Many times we wind up feeling better after exercising because our minds are given a break and are distracted from what we were worried about. Either we are forced to put our attention on something else or the exercise is repetitive enough that we can "move without thinking." Sometimes it is learning the steps to a new dance combination; other times we are focused on how we are lifting a particular weight, and often we are simply walking. Whatever the activity, it usually takes concentration to do it until eventually it does not. What I mean is that when we exercise, our brains have to accommodate the fact that we are moving, which causes a shift in our attention. I do not know about you, but after a while, I inevitably seem to reach a place where I am simply doing the activity and actually let go of whatever is on my mind. Later, after I have been distracted by whatever movement I have been doing, the answer to what I have been worried about seems to float up to my consciousness.

Consider the following low-impact physical activities when you're looking to shift your attention:

Pilates
Yoga
Ballet
Swimming
Nia
African dance

Understanding Our Unconscious Need for Movement

How we naturally move plus the different types of movement we are attracted to can help us understand who we are and what we need to ease our feelings of worry. Why do we feel the urge to run five miles or swim endless laps in a pool? What are our bodies trying to tell us? Probably more than we realize. I believe we have individual reasons for selecting the types of physical activity we do as well as universal reasons. We may not always be conscious of them, but if we take the time to explore why we are engaged in a specific form of exercise, we may be surprised at how the outside choice reflects an inside one. This realization was true for Trina, a young woman in her early thirties.

Trina arrived in my office to get support after her mother's death from cancer the year before. For a long time, she understandably had to process her deep feelings of grief in her therapy sessions. She also felt she needed to forge a new relationship with her father, to whom she had not felt close. After a period of time, Trina felt calmer and more stable in her life after working hard in therapy. She had gotten married and was busy in a new position in her industry.

Unexpectedly, tragedy struck again. Trina's father was diagnosed with lung cancer, and after battling the disease for a year, he passed away. Needless to say, Trina was devastated and deeply sad. She knew in her heart that she had healed many things with her father but found herself feeling lost in a world without either of her parents. She described herself as an orphan and shared with me that she felt shaky about her ability to make clear decisions. Trina worried that she would not be able to handle all the responsibilities that had piled up on her plate as she settled her father's estate.

EXERCISE FOR INNER AND OUTER STRENGTH

While Trina was processing her grief about her father in therapy, we began to talk about what she could do for herself outside her therapy sessions to feel more grounded. *Grounded* is a word that many people use to describe feeling both strong and solid in their sense of self. Trina needed to feel her inner strength and thought exercise would help. She found herself being drawn to Pilates and started taking a regular class twice a week. Much to her delight, she found that she absolutely loved it. When we talked about why she thought she enjoyed it so much, Trina told me that the class's emphasis on building core strength throughout the body was making her feel stronger as a person. "Not just physically," she told me, "but mentally as well. I am not worried that I can handle things, because I know I can. Even though I am sad, I feel more grown-up and less alone than before. I realize I can be my own person and that my parents are inside me forever." As she processed her grief, Trina's choice of exercise matched what she wanted to build within. The combination allowed her to remember her resourceful nature.

If we look at exercise as this thing we participate in just to burn calories or stay in shape, we limit how we can use movement to help us disengage from worry. On a most basic level, exercise is a stress reducer—and as Trina discovered, it can be even more. Physical activity will support you during times of worry and help you discover hidden aspects of your personality. You may find you love to dance, run, ride a bicycle, or go inline skating. As you master these new skills, your sense of vitality will grow. Both your mind and body will benefit from all you experience through movement. You will begin to see movement as a stress reliever. You want to engage in these activities because you like them rather than because you feel like you "have to."

Consider the following activities when you are trying to increase your inner strength as well as your outer strength:

Weight training
Kickboxing
Power walking
Martial arts
Yoga

Consider the following activities when you are trying to increase your balance:

Tai chi
Yoga
Pilates
Inline skating
Ballet

MATCHING MOVEMENT AND MOOD

As you discover what movement you enjoy or need, you may find that you are feeling and doing things differently. Your choice will be individual to each of you and will change periodically. Sometimes you will want to approach your worry with a quiet, methodical energy, and at other times you will attack what is bothering you with full physical force. Actually, either way will work if you do what you instinctively want to do. In addition, you usually will start to notice when you are craving something different. I know that when I am ready for something new in terms of exercise, I start to feel restless. I will notice that I am not as enthusiastic about attending a certain class or moving in a certain way. When my mother's illness was in a particularly stressful place, I moved away from power walking and started working with weights. I did not have a lot of energy to walk briskly, and I also wanted to feel more emotionally in charge. Like Trina, I really needed to feel that I was strong. Lifting weights helped me feel that and eased my worry.

How do you know what movement would help you with your worry? First, by taking the time to ask yourself what you might want to try, and second, by taking an action. Trina had never taken Pilates before, but she did feel drawn to it. If you feel like trying yoga, swimming, or dancing, go for it. Let your instinct guide you and then use your ongoing experience to help decide whether you would like to continue. You will also know whether you have chosen the right activity by noticing how you feel before, during, and after. The goal is to feel as if you have left something behind, hopefully your worries, and are returning to a calmer or more energized you. Whatever you try, aim for a sense of enjoyment and release afterward. If you do not feel that way, give yourself permission to explore other forms of physical movement. With physical activity, there are lots of opportunities to express or release whatever is causing us mental and emotional distress. You will become an expert in deducing what your body is telling you about how to de-stress once you start to apply your powers of observation.

Fitness expert and movement specialist for plus-sized women

Rochelle Rice knows a lot about this subject. Based in New York City, she is the author of *Real Fitness for Real Women* and travels across the United States speaking from her experience as a fitness professional. Rochelle and I have co-presented in numerous locations in the country on the topic of how emotion is held in the body and released through movement. We both observe the bodies of our patients and clients for clues and information about what traumas, worries, or emotional difficulties are being stored there. The human body and its innate knowledge use a language that can be learned for healing. Rochelle's philosophies are similar to mine. She brings years of experience to work with clients who have lost their own essential link to their bodies.

I asked Rochelle to share with me her observations about how her clients appear to her when they are worried. I also asked her to tell me how she saw movement's impact on the energy of worry. She said, "While the human physiology is more than capable to respond to worry with astonishing biomechanical changes, what I see many times in the body is that the stress and worry has been thwarted. The challenges of today repeatedly activate our stress response without any reprieve. What naturally defends our body during danger and worry now destroys our health in the long term." What Rochelle was noticing is the physical tension associated with worry and how her clients carry it in their bodies. That worry tension was not being let out and was held in her clients' bodies. I have seen the same thing in my office when my patients come in with something on their minds. Their expressions are cloudy and they are holding tension in various parts of their bodies such as their neck, shoulders, or lower back. I posed another question to Rochelle about how long, from her experience, it takes for movement and exercise to affect our mood once we get started. She said, "I believe you can shift or lessen someone's worry in as little as five or ten minutes even with just stretching and breathing." Imagine if you allowed yourself to move for even longer periods of time!

My colleague Tina Felluss, a licensed psychotherapist and workshop leader who works with cancer recovery and movement in a process called "Cancer Dancer," has seen this kind of shift firsthand. She shared an experience she had leading a movement workshop: "In one of my Transformational Nia classes, which is a combination dance/movement and fitness program, I had a new student. He claimed he had no rhythm and wouldn't be able to keep up with the group. He was right on one accord—he didn't have very much rhythm—but he kept up with the class beautifully, doing his own thing. At the end he said, 'I don't know what happened to me, but I was feeling stressed when I came in, and now my mind is calm and my body is relaxed.'"

I know that many of you can relate to his experience of feeling better after you have moved. Whether you have jogged, danced, or taken a walk, there is a feeling of release afterward. Tina concurred by saying, "Movement brings us into the body. We become aware of physical sensations and impulses that are continuously arising. By focusing on sensation, our thoughts become secondary—giving us the opportunity to 'switch gears.'" Again we see how using exercise and movement can apply directly to our worry. Whatever motion you choose, your mind will follow because a change is happening with your physical state. Eventually you will feel more relaxed and less burdened by your worrisome thoughts. If you need help choosing an activity I have created a description of possible emotional states, and Rochelle has provided a guide with the physical activities to match those emotional states. This list is a general one that can focus you toward what you may need when you are in a particular mood but do not know what to try.

If your emotional state/mood is anxious, agitated, nervous, angry, irritated, or a general feeling that you cannot relax, then you are a "fast worrier" and the following would be good for you:

- Hard-hitting movement, anaerobic exercise, large bursts of energy over short periods of time
- Running
- Boxing
- Weight lifting
- Outdoor sports
- Tennis

If your emotional state/mood is sad, blue, fearful, tearful, or a general feeling that you have no energy and need reassurance, then you are a "distressed worrier" and the following would be good for you:

- Flowlike movements
- Stretching
- Light yoga
- Walking
- Nia
- Swimming

Taking Those First Steps

As I wrote in Chapter 3, taking action disrupts the worry cycle. I believe the act of moving is one of the easiest actions to start if you are respectful of your fitness level when you first begin. Rochelle and I agree that when people need to move and do not feel comfortable in a formal fitness situation, one of the best actions they can do is to just start walking. With walking, you do not have to feel as if you are committed to any kind of exercise program. You are simply going to walk from one point to another at different times during the week. From there, you build a foundation by identifying the fact that you are moving all the time in life. Then you start to realize that there is movement in almost everything we do, whether it is carrying the laundry up and down the stairs, picking up children, or walking from the parking lot to your place of work. By refocusing your attention to your body's ability to take you places, you reaffirm the fact that we are meant to be mobile. We can then appreciate our body's capacity to influence our minds and vice versa and have more options to feel better.

DOING MOVEMENT YOU LIKE

If other things appeal to you besides walking, then try them as well. As Rochelle observed, "As a society, we seem to have lost the joy of movement and narrowed our choices to the gym. I invite people to expand to activities they may have learned as a child and movement they would like to do in the future. The body remembers what it was like to move worry-free and unencumbered by the stresses of adult life." So our movement is not relegated to the gym or a certain program, because it is happening all the time. Remember that how you are already moving counts, and then going forward you can start adding in things that you are drawn to. Maybe it is time to try belly dancing or water aerobics or tennis. My brother David keeps fit by playing softball in his community and loves the feeling of being outdoors. He gets to move his body and have fun at the same time. If you look at movement as an extension of your personality, you strengthen the link between your heart and head. You do what you enjoy, and your health reaps the benefits, too. This way you continue on with our body-mind-spirit theme because all movement is then a continuum rather than a start-and-stop process. When you allow yourself to go with the type of movement you *prefer* to do as opposed to what you think you *should* do, you affirm the instinctive part of yourself that knows what you need.

DETERMINING WHAT MOVEMENT IS RIGHT FOR YOU

In my book *Find Your Inner Voice*, I showed readers how to wake up their bodies and get their energy flowing through a series of exercises. The purpose was to help people notice, access, and apply their instinct and intuition. The more aware we are of our body's responses, the more insight we can use on a day-to-day basis. I have seen that once we connect to our bodies, we discover a wealth of information that we can use to improve our lives. The same holds true for managing your worry. The more you can move your body and get a sense of what works to alleviate your stress, the better you will feel. How can you tell what movement is right for you? First, I recommend taking the time to ask. Second, how about trying something to see how it feels? Here is an exercise that will help you begin to make your choice. (Read through the exercise first before you try it.)

Close your eyes and take a few deep breaths.

Starting at the top of your head, slowly focus on the different parts of your body, area by area. Focus on your head, neck, shoulders, arms, torso, back, hips, pelvis, thighs, hamstrings, knees, calves, shins, ankles, and feet.

Ask yourself: Where do my muscles feel tense?

What parts of my body feel like they need to move?

Is it my feet, legs, torso, hands, or arms?

How do those areas want to move?

If I could choose an activity right now that matches the way my body wants to move, what would it be?

Take a few more deep breaths, open your eyes, and note your observations.

What did you choose? Did your choice surprise you, or is it something you already participate in on a regular basis? Just know that the activity you are drawn to can either help you relieve your worry or end up being something you do for sheer enjoyment. Either way, your body and mind will thank you.

Moving Away from Worry When You're Not at Home

We aren't always in the comfort of our home when our worries and nagging, troublesome thoughts decide to invade our mind. The following are suggestions of activities that you can incorporate into your life while you're away from your home—at the office, visiting relatives, even on a plane.

IN THE OFFICE
To relieve excess tension or stress:

Cubicle or Wall Push-Ups
Stand with your hands against a flat surface, with your elbows bent. Do a series of push-ups against the wall, exhaling when you straighten your arms and inhaling when you bend them. Do about four or five push-ups, or more if necessary.

Jumping Jacks

Do ten jumping jacks in the office, in a conference room, or wherever you can find privacy. If jumping is a problem, you can step to the side with your right foot as you bring your arms up, then bring your left foot in as you bring your arms down to your sides. Then step to the side with your left foot. And so on.

Office Stretch

Stand with your knees slightly bent. Make a fist with each hand and place them on your lower back, just above your waist. Bring your knees together. Keep knees bent, bring them together so they are touching and slowly arch your back and let your neck gently drop back. Hold for about three to five seconds. Very slowly bring your head back up and straighten your body. Drop your arms to your sides and separate your knees. Inhale and slowly bend from the waist and let your head and arms dangle down toward the floor for about five seconds. Inhale deeply through your nose and then, as you exhale through your mouth, roll your body up until you are standing upright.

WHEN STAYING AT A HOTEL OR AT A FRIEND'S OR RELATIVE'S HOME

You can always do the preceding exercises away from home to relieve stress. If you need to relax and unwind you can also do the following:

Home-Away-from-Home Stretch

Lie on a bed with your knees bent, arms by your sides, palms down. (You can also put a pillow under your knees if your lower back is tight.) Inhale and slowly raise your pelvis toward the ceiling, using your hands for support, then exhale and bring your pelvis back down to the bed. Do this movement three or four times.

Spine Stretch

Lie on a bed or the floor with your knees bent, arms by your sides, palms down. Bring your knees to your chest and rest your hands on your knees. Inhale and slowly drop your knees to one side and let your arms spread out at shoulder level. Exhale. Inhale and exhale slowly two or three times. Inhale and bring your knees back up to your chest and do the same thing on the opposite side. When finished, roll to one side to bring yourself to a sitting position.

WHILE TRAVELING

Plane and Train Stretch

Inhale through your nose and slowly drop your chin to your chest. Exhale and bring your head back up. Inhale and then exhale, then slowly let your head drop back (do this slowly if your neck is tight). Inhale. Exhale and bring your neck back to center. Now inhale, turning your head to the left, then exhale and bring your head back to the center. Repeat and turn your head to the right and then back to the center. Do this series two or three times. After you have finished, inhale and raise your shoulders to your ears, hold them there for two or three seconds, and then exhale and drop them back to the normal position. Repeat this sequence two to four times.

Of course, be mindful of any physical limitations and check in with a trusted health practitioner before you start any new physical activities.

The Three Cs

Calmness

You have already explored where your body may be holding tension and what type of movement you may be craving. Without overthinking, ask yourself what physical activity would help relieve your worry and make you feel calmer. Do you imagine an activity that is high energy or one that is slow moving? When you picture yourself engaging in that activity, how do you feel? How about when you visualize yourself finished? Can you fit that movement into your schedule over the next few days or weeks? If you already are moving your body on a regular basis, do you need any changes or does it feel just right? If everything is fine, keep going. If not, maybe it is time to seek a different fitness level or start something new.

Clarity

Through the exploration of unconscious movement you can discover what lies behind physical tension. As you become more aware of the places your body may be holding tension, use that information to create an inner dialogue. What is your body trying to tell your mind through all the little aches, pains, and stiffness you experience? Again, if no medical issues are involved, there may be some emotional information for you to discover. The question I like to ask is, "If that body part could talk, what would it want me to know?" Once you have that knowledge, you will have the clarity you need to decide what to do.

Community

As you have gotten to know yourself over the past few chapters, you have probably discovered how you like to learn. If you have not done so already, you can always review the questionnaire on page 30 in Chapter 1. With this information, you will be able to turn to resources, classes, and experts for guidance. You may like taking a solitary walk or dancing with a group. You may enjoy working one-on-one with a trainer or teacher in order to absorb a new movement technique or exercise. Maybe a DVD or video gets your energy flowing every day. No matter what the source, tapping into the wealth of knowledge out there in the fitness/movement arena will give you the tools you need to move your body.

How you naturally move and the different types of movement you are drawn to will help you reclaim your body and reduce your worry. When you allow yourself to move daily, your mind and mood will eventually start to respond. The more you move in the way that matches who you are and what you need, the better you will feel. Of course, now that we have looked at how to exercise our bodies for optimum enjoyment and worry reduction, it is time to learn how to fuel them. After all, moving around requires us to expend energy, and we need to make sure we are giving ourselves good nutritional options in order to keep going.

CHAPTER SIX

Food and Mood

In this chapter, we will examine how food can be either our friend or foe when it comes to managing our worry. We will examine what lies beneath our food choices and how emotions, such as worry, can create problems in our eating habits. We will also focus on how those foods can affect our overall mood. The purpose of exploring your food choices is not to judge your eating habits but to offer insight on how what you choose to eat can both contribute to and reduce the effects of worry. I have even asked a few nutrition experts to offer their expertise on how particular foods affect our mood. They will provide information and suggestions for you that will help you maintain your physical energy, support your mental clarity, and keep your spirits balanced, to better enable you to handle life's difficulties.

When Worried Meets Sugar and Caffeine

I remember a patient I had many years ago, a young man who was physically active and had no issues with food. During our treatment together, he broke up with his girlfriend and worried whether he would ever find another relationship. He shared in therapy that he found himself eating a pint of ice cream every night when he got home from work. This was unusual behavior for this patient, who normally liked to go to the gym after he left the office. He told me he was not feeling in the mood to work out after work and instead found himself heading straight to his apartment and later to his freezer. When we explored this behavior, he discovered that underneath all the ice cream was a great deal of sadness. Eating the ice cream was his way of soothing his feelings and providing comfort over the loss of his relationship. Once he was able to connect to those feelings, his desire for his nighttime treat diminished. He later told me that the ice cream was "not doing the trick anyway," and in reality the nightly pints were making him feel sluggish in the morning. As he felt better, he returned to his usual ways of taking care of himself through exercise and connecting to friends.

When we are worried and stressed, our bodies go into the hyper state of arousal I described in Chapter 1. That was the fight-or-flight response we have in reaction to perceived danger. This means that all of our internal systems and organs are focused on how to handle whatever is causing us to be on high alert. As the result of excess stress, our bodies start to produce the hormones adrenaline and cortisol, which are both secreted by the adrenal glands. These small kidney-shaped glands kick out a surge of power when we need it, so that we have the extra boost of energy we need in order to handle a crisis. That crisis can be large (such as running from a fire), small (such as having to finish a school paper), or ongoing (such as caring for someone with a chronic illness). Whatever the size of the crisis, the adrenal glands will continue their output of adrenaline. Adrenaline increases our heart rate, elevates our blood pressure, and generally speeds up our energy. We use adrenaline when responding to perceived danger, and it enables us to make quick decisions. After the danger has passed, your body returns to a state of calm and your hormone levels go back to normal.

Imagine what your body is going through when you are in a constant state of worry and when you are physically tense. The adrenal glands try to do their job by responding with a continual release of adrenaline. If your state of worry never shifts, the adrenals will keep supplying adrenaline. Over time, the adrenal glands are overworked by such continual overuse and do not function as well. This constant stress affects your body's overall ability to cope. A domino effect starts to occur because if we do not have properly functioning adrenals, we feel tired. When we feel this fatigue, we may turn to quick sources of energy, such as caffeine and sugar, to keep going. Because the effects of those foods are short-lived, and they give us a fast boost but not a sustained one, we turn to them again and again. Soon, we find ourselves on a physical and ultimately emotional roller coaster of needing energy, looking for a quick fix, and then crashing physically when the sugar and caffeine wear off.

The same holds true for the hormone cortisol. Cortisol is also released by the adrenal glands and is used to manage the stress response in the body. Cortisol helps keep your immune system balanced, regulates your blood pressure, and keeps in check any of your other internal systems that are not needed when you are responding to a suspected threat. However, when you are in a chronic state of stress and do not return to a more relaxed state, too much cortisol is produced and has nowhere to go. Over time, the excess cortisol starts to work against you. Among other things, excess cortisol causes weight gain, impairs your memory, and affects your thyroid function. Until the real cause of the problem—chronic worry—is addressed, a cycle begins to happen. We end up choosing foods to keep going in the short term as opposed to making changes that will support us in the long term.

The Food and Worry Connection

When someone starts to gain or lose weight and there is no medical issue, it can usually be attributed to the stresses of life, which people respond to by over- or undereating. These stresses can include a variety of issues such as job worries, money worries, relationship problems, and family demands. Many people who tend to overeat turn to food for comfort, to reduce anxiety, to stuff anger, or to push beyond their exhaustion. Unless the reasons for overeating are understood, the person's use of food to *manage feelings* will continue until they reach a point of ill health, have gained weight, or feel exhausted and emotional.

These symptoms are the body's way of presenting its bill for food being used as a coping mechanism. The use of excess food to cope develops for many psychological and emotional reasons. Over time, eating becomes a way to manage uncomfortable feelings from either the past or the present. Food becomes an area where that tension plays out and can cause quite a bit of emotional distress. Until there is an understanding, release, and resolution to what you are feeling, the choice to manage emotions through overeating will happen again.

As a therapist, I know that most people do not *want* to turn to unhealthy behaviors to cope and are sometimes not even aware that the urge to eat poorly is connected to either a state of worry or other emotional issues. In fact, those who struggle with compulsive or binge eating often describe it as an overwhelming need. They feel compelled to engage in these behaviors and are not really conscious about why they are eating when they are not hungry. Afterward, when they feel lousy from the unhealthy food choices or have gained weight, they inevitably feel ashamed and helpless about their inability to remain in control.

The same holds true for those who undereat. As we saw

when looking at stress hormones earlier, if we are continually worried and stressed, our appetite can actually get suppressed. When I first heard the news about my mother's diagnosis, I could not eat for a few days. I just was not interested and spent most of my time trying to digest the news. As I researched more about our stress hormones, I saw how my reaction fit right into human biology. When our bodies are on alert and focused on a problem, the internal systems that are not needed shut down for a while. I imagine it is similar to when we put our computers into sleep mode. They are still on but not fully functioning until we need them to. So, loss of appetite due to chronic worry keeps us from getting what we really need, which is good, healthy sources of energy. Over time the lack of nutrients takes its toll on our bodies, moods, and perspectives. Parents know from experience how feeding hungry children can take them from tears to laughter. This is a good example of how acutely our moods are affected when we are deprived, even for a short time, of nourishment.

Food, Worry, and Reality Checking

Kay was a young woman in her late thirties who was a vice president in a public-relations firm. Married for about four years, Kay came for therapy because she was very unhappy with her physical appearance. Over the past five years Kay had steadily been gaining weight and had put on about thirty pounds. She told me she was not sure why she was gaining weight and said, "I'm definitely not the most healthy eater, but I don't feel I eat that much."

After exploring Kay's history with food and ruling out any eating disorders, I had her describe a typical week. Kay revealed that she was a social person on the weekends with a fairly demanding schedule during the week. She explained that she tended to eat at odd hours because of her job and often used food to either wind down or rev up. She usually arrived home around ten P.M., and because she had not eaten enough earlier in the day, she ended up ordering food and drinking wine to relax. She would then fall asleep around one A.M. after watching television. In the morning, because she was exhausted, she had numerous cups of coffee to get going plus whatever sugary pastry appealed to her. In a basic way, Kay was addressing her long days and fatigue in the short term by giving her body what it craved. The sugar and coffee gave her energy, whereas the wine and late dinners helped her wind down. Yet as Kay and I discovered, the long-term solution was about addressing the real issue: her demanding job.

Kay believed that if she did not stay late and keep herself available to her staff, she would be viewed as slacking off. Kay's yearly reviews had always been positive, so her perspective on her job seemed off. I encouraged Kay to start setting some more realistic boundaries around her work hours and to create more time to be with her husband.

In order to help Kay verify her perspective and keep her

from worrying, I asked her to get a reality check for each action she took. She could do this in two ways: checking in either before she took an action or after. For example, Kay decided to let her boss know that she was going to start leaving the office earlier. She discovered that her boss was not aware that Kay had been staying so late and supported her wholeheartedly. The second option involved Kay getting a reality check after she began shutting her office door for periods of time either to catch up on her own work or to eat lunch. When she tried it, she realized that her staff could handle things when she was not there to answer questions and that they could wait until she was available. More important, Kay got back the time she needed for herself. These two actions had a direct effect on her weight and energy. By eating lunch when she was hungry, carving out her own time in her office, and reducing her hours, Kay was able to make better food choices. Over the course of a year, she slowly lost the weight she had gained. The combination of reality checking and eating on a regular basis helped stabilize her body and mind.

These kinds of adjustments, along with good food choices, are going to help us ride the waves of worry. As we have seen throughout this book, bringing awareness to when our eating patterns went awry is a first step toward getting back on track. Remember, it is important when you are doing any kind of self-examination to be both conscious and compassionate. That means recognizing that things need to change but not berating yourself for making poor choices because of worry or fear. When we need to make changes, we have to be on our own side—that is, be our own best advocate as we take steps forward.

Food Clues

If you are struggling with your food choices, look at the following questions to see if you can pinpoint when and why your eating habits changed. Take a few deep inhales and exhales before you begin.

- When did you start to notice your eating habits begin to change?
- When did you first notice it?
- How long ago was it?
- What time of year or month was it?
- Can you remember what events were happening during that time?
- Describe those circumstances. Were they personal or professional?
- What was your response at that time to those situations?
- As you think about it now, how are you feeling?
- Is there something you need to address or change now that would help you feel better?
- What would that be?

You can always go to the Three Cs section of this chapter and look at them to help you come up with some solutions if you need them. If you find yourself in the middle of a bad eating or drinking episode and want to put on the brakes quickly, look at the following four-step method. I created this technique to help people take back control when their behavior was feeling out of control. This process will help you make the connection between what you are choosing and what you are feeling.

Time to Get S.A.N.E.

If you realize that you tend to use food to manage your worry, and you are not hungry, consider using this step-by-step process to help you break that automatic behavior. You can post this on your desk, on your refrigerator, or in your car to use as a quick way to hit the pause button when you need it.

S—Stop

Stop whatever you are doing for a minute, five minutes, or even an hour. Simply give yourself the space to catch your breath and take a break. If you are in the middle of an eating or drinking binge, take some time away from the activity and literally change rooms or locations. You can always go back to the behavior if you want to. Even if you are not feeling out of control, taking a breather is a nice way to reconnect with yourself. Whether you are waiting to pick up your kids, sitting at a desk, or commuting on the train, take a moment for yourself. Try some slow deep breathing, listen to soothing music, or just shut your eyes.

A—Acknowledge

If you are feeling out of control with food or drink, acknowledge that something is going on in your life that is causing you to cope by overdoing it. When we consciously think about our actions, they become choices as opposed to something happening *to us*. Maybe the current choice is not *the* healthiest or most caring, but it is the choice we are making in this moment to handle a stressful or worrisome event or person in our life. If possible, jot down some of the situations or issues you are currently dealing with. Ask yourself what you are thinking or feeling about these situations. Examine whether there is a link between what you are trying to manage and your desire to overeat.

N—Normalize

Normalize the fact that you have chosen food to manage your emotions and stress. Instead of beating yourself up, recognize that you, and many others, choose the same coping mechanism. This coping mechanism, which is a learned and familiar reaction, is one that you automatically turn to when you are stressed. You are not a bad person for responding to worry by overeating or drinking, you are just relying on a comfortable and familiar short-term solution to a problem or issue that feels overwhelming. Once you realize that you are not an oddity but one of many who respond the same way, you move from a place of helplessness to a place of strength.

E—Evaluate

As you become aware of what you are feeling and how you are responding to it, you can evaluate what you need. This allows you to address whatever you are worried about using more long-term solutions. These answers may include sharing your feelings, revising your busy schedule, or perhaps taking some time off. Use this self-reflection time to review what would help you release the mental and emotional stress you are under. When you create the space to breathe, feel, and think, you have a better chance of discovering what you need. As always, if you feel that the issue you are dealing with and how you are responding to it is beyond your ability to control, make sure you reach out and get professional support.

Remember, the body-mind connection is a strong and powerful resource for you to access. The more conscious you make the link between your worry and your food choices, the more information you will receive on what you require to break the cycle of overindulgence. Once you have that knowledge, you will be able to create different and healthier options. Let's now take a more specific look at what types of foods can support you during times of worry.

The Power of Food

I conferred with two nutritional experts—Jeanette Bronee, CHHC, AADP, and Martha McKittrick, R.D., CDE—on the subject of worry and food. Jeanette Bronee is a nourishment counselor, a hypnotherapist, and the president and owner of the Path for Life Self-Nourishment Center in New York City. Jeanette uses a holistic approach to how we nourish our bodies and believes that when our bodies and minds are nourished, we are better able to handle many more of life's responsibilities. As Jeanette and I discussed food and mood, I was curious how our metabolism was affected by worry and stress. Because one of the physical responses of our body is to release adrenaline and cortisol, I wanted to understand how those hormones affect our body's processing of food. Jeanette explained to me that when our adrenaline and cortisol levels rise, our digestive process is slowed. She said, "Basically, back in the day when we were first 'designed,' it was all about survival, so we could not be stressing and digesting at the same time. Therefore the bodily processes take care of what is most important first." This brought to my mind the image of our early ancestors running from a predator, which usually meant they were not holding an ice cream cone!

Of course, we now live in modern times, which means eating on the run, at our desks, or not at all. So many of us aren't in a relaxed state when we eat, and our ability to digest food is affected. We can't effectively process and absorb what we need to from our food. Our metabolism slows and can end up storing that excess energy as weight. According to Jeanette, when our stress hormones are affected, so is our entire system. She said, "We may not feel hungry because of our stress, but when we sit down at the end of the day after waiting so long to eat, our hormones 'tell us' to binge. That is actually a normal and hormonally designed post-stress reaction."

What We Crave

I do not usually find myself grabbing broccoli and eating salads when I feel overwhelmed. No, I'm more likely to be seen with candy or coffee in my hand. Jeanette confirmed that because our cortisol levels rise in response to our worry, so do our insulin levels. This increase in insulin levels triggers our craving for more sugar- and carbohydrate-rich foods. It reminds me of a patient I once had who lived on sugary cookies and candy. When we explored this issue, she made the connection between the lack of affection in her personal relationship and her need for some sweetness. I found her words very poignant because she was literally trying to sweeten her love life and had found a short-term solution. I've observed in my work with patients with eating disorders that sugar also tends to be a big binge food, as it tends to shift our moods or numb our feelings.

We also may choose a comforting meal when we come home at the end of a stressful day. Comfort foods are soft in texture, such as creamy mashed potatoes, pudding, or foods high in starch and simple carbohydrates such as cookies or bread. The instinctive desire for these types of foods is physiological. Carbohydrates cue the brain to make serotonin, a neurotransmitter that has a calming effect in the body. This hormone is our "feel good" hormone, and low levels of it can cause us to feel sad or depressed. Serotonin is also thought to give us that satisfied feeling from food and help promote sleep and relaxation. Although it is certainly okay to have a comforting meal at the end of the day, the types of foods we put into that meal can affect us over the next few days. I've had patients tell me they feel sluggish, tired, or bloated when they have eaten too many cookies or high-fat and salty foods such as chips or fried foods. Our body's reaction becomes a clear indicator when something we have eaten is not helping our health.

What to Reach For

Jeanette recommends more complex carbs instead of the simple ones mentioned earlier to help us calm down. She suggests we choose foods such as whole grains and vegetables instead of processed bread, pasta, and cookies.

Supermarkets today are stocking many more complex-carbohydrate items for us to buy for ourselves and our families. The result of eating these foods is that because they are rich in complex carbohydrates they are broken down more slowly, causing increased stability of our blood sugar levels. This stability provides us with a steadier, more even flow of energy, which is what we really need to help us cope with our worry.

According to Jeanette, "We get fuel from complex carbs and good-quality fats, which are important. Whole wheat, oats, brown rice, and root vegetables such as sweet potatoes, carrots, beets, and turnips provide us with slow, steady energy. Olive oil, avocados, and nuts nourish our skin and nails plus make us feel full and satisfied. When we eat foods of a more complex nature (whole foods), our brain functions better. The problem is that we have learned to choose fat-free foods, which causes us to crave more sugar as a source of energy." I could not agree more. When we don't have enough fat to feel satisfied, we tend to eat more of the fat-free foods, looking for the satisfaction that fats give us.

Protein is great for producing energy, but it does take energy to digest, which is why some of us get tired after a meal. Protein affects our dopamine levels—which is our "take action" hormone. Dopamine, like serotonin, is defined as both a neurotransmitter and a hormone. Having adequate protein is important for energy, and where you choose to get it is an individual choice. Many vegetarians know how to get their protein from plant sources and are as healthy as their meat-eating friends. All in all, it appears that the quartet of hormones adrenaline, cortisol, serotonin, and dopamine is very important to how we process foods. I find it interesting how complex yet interrelated the systems in our bodies are and how they keep us healthy.

Martha McKittrick is a registered dietitian and certified diabetes educator in New York City specializing in nutritional counseling for the person with a busy schedule. Martha knows firsthand how our food choices affect our mood, our energy levels, and our immune system, which can help the body fight the effects of stress caused by worry. Meanwhile, bad food can drain the body. Martha suggests limiting caffeine and alcohol. She says, "Caffeine has a direct effect on the brain and nervous system. Because caffeine and stress can both elevate cortisol levels, high amounts of caffeine can exacerbate the effects of stress in the body, leading to prolonged elevated levels of cortisol. While small to moderate amounts of caffeine can lift your mood and give you a boost, excessive amounts can make you jittery and on edge." She goes on to say, "Many of us also get the urge to turn to 'the bottle' when stress levels rise. However, this can actually be the worst thing you can do. Excess alcohol adds further stress to the body by lowering our immune system, leaving us vulnerable to flu and seasonal illness. Alcohol disrupts our sleep by not allowing us to drop deeply into a restful sleep the way we need to. On top of that, alcohol also adds empty calories to our diet."

You've just received a lot of information on how our food choices affect our mood, behavior, and immunity. But I bet you'd love a more complete breakdown of what foods are good for the worrier who needs to calm down, the worrier who needs energy, and the worrier who needs to build their defenses. I also bet you'd love a list that tells you what foods to avoid. Today is your lucky day, because I have asked Martha and Jeanette to help me out in creating the right lists for you.

Foods That Calm and Help Achieve Balance

Fatty fish: salmon, mackerel, bluefish, and herring
Anchovies
Ground flaxseed
Walnuts
Raspberries and strawberries

Free-range beef and poultry
Wheat germ
Kidney and navy beans
Broccoli and cauliflower

Whole Foods That Help Maintain Energy and Push Out Toxins

Whole-grain cereals and breads
Whole-wheat pasta
Brown rice
Legumes
Fresh fruit
Fresh vegetables
Oats
Millet
Barley

Energy-Rich Foods That Sustain

Lean protein: turkey, chicken, fish, and legumes
Fresh fruit: oranges, berries, melons, grapes, pears, and apples
Nuts: almonds, walnuts, pecans, and pistachios
Fresh fruit and vegetable juices: beet, carrot, cucumber, tomato, apple, pear, orange, watermelon, and so on
Smoothies made from fruit, soy milk, rice milk, or low-fat milk or yogurt

Green drinks made from spinach, wheatgrass, parsley, celery, or spirulina

Magnesium-Rich Foods That Prevent Stress Hormones from Rising

Legumes: peas, beans, lentils, soy, and peanuts
Nuts: almonds, cashews, peanuts, and Brazil nuts
Whole grains: brown rice, barley, wild rice, millet, and quinoa
Green vegetables: spinach, kale, okra, and broccoli
Pumpkin seeds

Antioxidant-Rich Foods That Bolster Our Immunity

Beta-carotene: apricots, asparagus, beets, broccoli, cantaloupe, carrots, corn, green peppers, kale, mangoes, turnip and collard greens, nectarines, peaches, pink grapefruit, pumpkin, squash, spinach, sweet potato, tangerines, tomatoes, and watermelon
Vitamin C: berries, broccoli, brussels sprouts, cantaloupe, cauliflower, grapefruit, honeydew, kale, kiwi, mangoes, nectarines, oranges, and papaya
Vitamin E: wheat germ, nuts, safflower oil, soybean oil, mangoes, chard, mustard, and turnips
Zinc: oysters, red meat, poultry, beans, nuts, seafood, whole grains, fortified cereals, and dairy products

Selenium: Brazil nuts, tuna, beef, poultry, fortified breads, and other grain products

Foods to Avoid or Limit

Caffeine

Alcohol

Fat-free/diet foods made with processed or artificial ingredients

The Three Cs

Calmness

In a previous chapter, we looked at how moving your body relieves worry and takes you into a calmer state. In this chapter, we have seen a direct link between what we eat and how we feel. As you think about the way you want to move your body, imagine the type of food that would support the energy needed for that movement. Vigorous exercise usually calls for a heartier kind of fuel. Other times, when our exercise is slower-moving, we may want lighter foods. In general, when we are worried, we want to choose foods that give us sustained energy when we need it and foods that help us unwind when we need to calm down. Fuel your body with the nutrition you need to keep you as balanced as possible during times of stress.

Keep raising your awareness in regard to the effects of good, healthy food on your mood.

Clarity

As you continue to fine-tune your body-mind connection, you will gain knowledge about what you need in regard to your food choices. Keep checking in with yourself to see if you are operating in your life the way you want to be. Are you making habitual, short-term choices for situations that may require deeper examination? Are there changes that need to occur so that you let go of some poor eating habits? Is your thinking clear, or do you feel fuzzy from too much sugar or highly processed foods? Are you able to make decisions from a place of clarity, or does what you eat make you feel unclear about what you want to do? Trust that your body will let you know fairly quickly whether what you are providing is supportive.

Community

There are many different paths to making better nutritional choices. Knowing who we are and how we like to utilize resources will help us find our way. You want to consider all of the sources that make sense to you to help you make healthier decisions. Think about the people you know who are taking good care of themselves and ask them for advice. Investigate books and articles that offer nutritional advice that you can relate to. Look around for groups or classes that offer guidance in food and health. Know that there are experts in your community, like my colleagues mentioned in this chapter, who can help you get started and support you along the way. Remember that you can make step-by-step changes, and even little shifts will make a difference in how you cope with worry.

The journey toward healthier eating is not about being perfect. As we have seen, we often make poor choices because we are worried and preoccupied about what to do about certain issues and difficulties we are managing. We try to keep going when maybe we need to stop and regroup. We comfort ourselves with foods that serve us in the short term, but in the long run we end up betraying our bodies. Fortunately we have wonderful brains to help think things through and good, bodily instinct for when we have gone too far. The more we cultivate our body-mind awareness, the better our nutritional decisions will be. So far, we have investigated how adding movement and making wiser food choices help us reduce worry. Now let us see how adding a good night's sleep into the mix will help us further reduce worry.

CHAPTER SEVEN

Hard Day's Night

We met my friend Sharon in Chapter 1. She is the one who reported being sleepless in Manhattan for many months. At that time, Sharon had called me to see if I had any information on holistic methods for sleep. She shared that she was able to fall asleep, but intermittent periods of waking up through the night had left her frazzled and exhausted. She found herself relying more and more on a prescribed sleep aid but was feeling uncomfortable with the lingering effect it had on her the following day. Sharon told me she was unable to participate in all the activities she enjoyed because she did not feel up to it. Besides feeling tired, she found that she was irritable and emotional about things that normally would not bother her.

I understand how she feels. When I don't get enough sleep, my overall perspective becomes distorted and I feel a bit thin-skinned in response to different circumstances around me. My friends who are parents tell me they observe the same thing with their overly tired children. Until the kids get their naps, they are often inconsolable about seemingly minor issues. As grown-ups we can usually push through our fatigue, but I believe that a bunch of cranky, sleep-deprived three-year-olds are probably hidden beneath that adult façade, myself included. Catching up on my sleep usually helps me with my view of life, and I suspect the same holds true for others. But what if, like Sharon, the catching-up part doesn't happen often enough?

Worry and Sleep

This chapter focuses on the connection between worry and how it affects our ability to get enough sleep. We will explore what keeps us up at night, and techniques to help you transition from your daily stress to nightly relaxation will be provided. We will learn some exercises that will help you put to bed what is troubling you and find some practical tips on how to get better sleep in general. Understanding what it means to rest, unwind, and release mental and physical tension will be an important part of the process. In addition, I've asked a feng shui expert for suggestions on how to set up your bedroom so that you can enjoy a calming atmosphere where you sleep. You will also explore whether you need additional support beyond self-discovery.

Most of us spend one-third of our lives sleeping. That can be hard to imagine when so many of us are struggling to even fall asleep. Nearly everyone I know complains about being tired all the time. Whether it is caused by the worry of being a new mom or dad, the worry over job security that has us working long hours, or the worry of taking care of elderly parents, it seems that a lot of us are simply not getting enough sleep. According to the National Sleep Foundation, most people these days are getting an average of seven hours of sleep per night. Yet we seem to be spending longer hours at the office and are busier than ever managing our family's schedule. Add worry to this mix and things get really out of balance.

Why is sleep so important? According to recent research, sleep is an important biological function that allows us to review our day and improves the way we process memories. We need to sleep for a certain number of hours in order to recharge our bodies and support our brains. That number is individual to all of us. So why does it seem that everything we are worried about gets amplified at night? Just at the time when we need to wind down, we find ourselves wound up. For some, it may be that when the day is done, there is space to let those worries bubble to the surface. For other folks, it could be because daytime business blends into the night and peaks when they are the most exhausted. No matter what the cause, it seems that our special time for rest gets nibbled away bit by bit by worrisome matters in the mind. Sharon learned this as well.

As Sharon explored different medical and behavioral methods to address her sleeplessness, she discovered a big connection to worry. Beneath her tossing and turning lay a low-grade worry about her ability to maintain a business she had built from scratch. As I mentioned in Chapter 1, though Sharon was holding her own, her business had taken a hit because of the economy. She felt vulnerable and sometimes doubted her ability to keep her business thriving. As she began to lose sleep, her fears became heightened. Sharon needed to take action—and she did.

First, Sharon ruled out any serious medical issues that might be affecting her sleep through a series of doctor appointments, starting with her primary care physician. She wanted to know if any physical systems within her body were out of balance. After finding out that she was basically okay, she decided to try a natural supplement called melatonin, known for helping with sleep, while weaning herself off her prescribed sleep aid. To her surprise, she found that she could fall asleep without the sleeping pill, eliminating the next-day drug hangover that usually occurred. It is important to note that Sharon did not do all of this abruptly. She did her research. First she spoke with her doctor, who supported her in going off her sleeping aid, and then she thoroughly researched some alternatives. She made mature, informed decisions regarding supplements and medications based on what she felt would work for her. She did not haphazardly add or subtract things without fully understanding how to do so. I mention this because it is extremely important to be fully informed and responsible for any actions we take regarding our health. Knowledge and personal choice are important pillars for maintaining your health.

As the final part of Sharon's journey, she decided to speak with a therapist and discover her real reason for her sleeplessness. As she sorted through her feelings about her career, Sharon realized that some of her worries were legitimate and some were not. Her real worry was about the dip in the economy and how that would affect her financially. Remember how we explored in Chapter 1 whether stress is ever a good thing? In Sharon's case, her stress signaled that something in her business needed to be looked at. Sometimes stress is based on real issues that we must address and helps us pay attention to them. Sharon realized that she could probably keep a better eye on her business budget and make better efforts to drum up more clients. The thought of taking that action actually made her feel more in charge.

Her unfounded worries had to do with old insecurities about having her own business to begin with. These insecurities occurred because before she started her business, Sharon had held a secure job with a successful company. She has done very well on her own, but every once in a while old negative thoughts would creep up about the wisdom of leaving a secure position to try something new. I have heard versions of this in my practice over the years and have gone through it myself. Those are the times when we look around our new office, home, or country and ask, "What have I done?" Most of the time we have probably done the very thing we needed to do, but with change comes vulnerability, and it is normal to experience doubt. Sharon realized this about her own worries. She recognized that her old thoughts were just that: old and unrealistic. Once she reminded herself that she had taken care of herself and could continue to do so, her sleep improved even more.

Putting Worries to Bed

How can you put your worries to bed so you can sleep? You have a few options. The first is to try sharing your concerns with someone as you wind down for the night. Can you talk to a friend, loved one, or significant other? Again, from experience, the earlier in the evening you do this, the better, but there is nothing wrong with a midnight heart-to-heart if the other person is literally up for it. Try to identify what you need from this person. Sometimes we want advice, and sometimes we just want a pair of ears to listen. Think about what you may need before you reach out.

As my husband, Michael, can attest, I have a teeny, tiny little habit of bringing up things I am concerned about right before we go to bed. Of course, because I am tired, my perspective about what is bothering me is not very accurate. I start fretting about one thing and end up globalizing about where I am headed in life and the future. I tend to throw whatever is on my mind into the worry mix. Michael will usually pause a moment, look at me, and say, "You know what, sweetheart? Now is not the time. Why don't you put it away for now and we will talk about it tomorrow?" I have to tell you, it works almost every time. On some level I know it is not the right time, and I feel a bit of relief that my worry cycle is being stopped. And because I know I always have the option to talk about my worries the next day, I feel that I can relax knowing that I can air them at another time. I am able to put my worries away for the night. Of course, by the next day, I usually have a more balanced perspective.

It also helps to write down your worries in your worry journal. When you put your thoughts down on paper or on-screen, you have the opportunity to clear your mind and leave the worries behind. And if you are still experiencing sleep troubles and have ruled out any medical issues, it is time to get creative. It sometimes helps to picture your worries leaving your head and imagine locking them away for the night.

Worry Journal Before Bed

- Try some of the exercises we looked at in previous chapters, which will help pinpoint your concerns. Look at the worry journal discussion on pages 57–66.
- Try the logic exercises on pages 99–101.
- Write in a journal style, which means putting down everything that is on your mind without censoring it. With this style of writing, you can discover what is on your mind and find answers as they come to you. This is particularly helpful when what you are worried about cannot be addressed through a plan of action. Writing journal style allows you to leave your worries on the page, which helps you let them go, at least for now.
- Create a list of your worries and rank them in order of concern. Then you can create a plan to address the most important one first and go down the list from there.

Using a step-by-step approach can make you feel less anxious.

▪ If the worry that is keeping you up concerns the possibility of future events such as a security threat or a natural disaster, you can use the preparation and information approach we discussed on pages 30–32. Make a list of where you will go for solid information and remind yourself that once you have it, you can prepare in the way that makes you feel safe.

▪ If you are a visual person, draw, sketch, and doodle your worries on paper. Use colors and imagery to capture your worries and use your artistic imagination to figure out or dissolve those worrisome images.

▪ Write a letter you will never send and address it to whomever you need spiritual guidance from. Ask for the wisdom and support you need to let go of your worries. You can also read your letter out loud and then put it, and your worries, away for the night.

Activate Your Imagination

▪ As you are lying in bed, close your eyes and imagine a container that you associate with a feeling of safety, peacefulness, and calm. This container can be any shape, color, or size. It may have many details associated with it, or it may be plain and simple. You may recognize it from the past or create it from scratch.

▪ Imagine each worry that you have being put into the

container. You could picture yourself putting your worries in one by one or see them streaming into the opening of the container. Envision this happening until all your worries are in the container.

- Now picture the top of the container being shut for the night. You can close it any way you want. You can put a lock on it, shut the top with a see-through door, or cover the container with a colorful or vivid piece of cloth. Remind yourself that your worries are contained for the night and that you can always take them out again in the morning.

- Imagine putting the container in a safe place.

- Ask yourself if there is anything else you need to do; if not, see if you can go to sleep.

NIGHTTIME ROUTINE

Remember when we were younger and bedtime rolled around? No matter what time it was, it was always too early to go to sleep. Yet most of us probably had an established time that we went to bed. We also may remember a series of activities leading up to bedtime that were pretty much the same every night. Those of you who are parents are familiar with your own set of activities that help you put your children to bed at night. My friend Rebecca has two young children and after dinner, her two kids usually watch a short video of one their favorite characters from PBS. Then they have a bath, brush their teeth, and use the bathroom, and she reads them a final story. I have been at her house when she puts her kids to bed, and they do seem quite comfortable and secure about going to sleep.

As adults, we may have some version of a routine before we go to bed, but perhaps it is not so soothing. Many of us wind down after long days with television of varying content, maybe spend time on the computer, and then attempt to go to sleep. Yet with our long hours, we probably are eating and drinking later and staying up long after we are actually ready for bed. In my practice, I have noticed that most people do not have enough transition time before they go to sleep. We shut off the television after watching intense or violent content and jump straight into bed. Or sometimes we take a phone call and engage in a lengthy, upsetting conversation before climbing into bed. I know people for whom the last thing they do before going to bed is check their BlackBerry, and some fall asleep on a full stomach, all of which affects our quality of sleep. An action-packed television show or difficult conversation may make us tense. Work issues may force us to stay awake longer than we need to and worry about how we'll get everything done.

GETTING GOOD ZZZZ

The National Sleep Foundation recommends ways to create an atmosphere that is conducive to relaxation and quality sleep. According to the National Sleep Foundation, we should do the following:

- Maintain a regular bedtime and wake-up time.
- Establish a regular, relaxing bedtime routine.

- Create a sleep-conducive environment.
- Finish eating at least two to three hours before your regular bedtime.
- Exercise regularly.
- Avoid caffeine close to bedtime.
- Avoid alcohol close to bedtime.

Maintain a Regular Bedtime and Wake-Up Time

The National Sleep Foundation recommends a regular bedtime and wake-up time. This is based on their research showing that our body and brain need to maintain a balance between rest and alertness. In my opinion, it may take a little exploring to discover your natural bedtime and wake-up time. Some of us require less sleep than others, and how you feel when you wake up will be a key piece of information. If you are going to bed at a certain time and waking up refreshed and alert, then you probably are getting enough sleep. If you are struggling to get up and feel tired through most of your day, you may have to make some adjustments.

A good time to experiment with wake and sleep times is on the weekend or on vacation. On a night when you are not out late but simply going to bed when you are tired, see what time you wake up without the alarm. Notice how many hours of sleep you got and track the average. Many people already know how much they need and will say emphatically that they need eight or even ten hours a night. Others say that they do not need more than six. We are all different, and observing your energy levels during the day compared to your amount of sleep will be helpful. Obviously for new parents or those in special-care circumstances, this may be difficult. My recommendation in those cases is to grab sleep whenever you can and when your body tells you that you need to.

Establish a Bedtime Routine

As I cared for my mom, I got a chance to watch her night-time routine quite often and it rarely varied. Even though her memory was affected, she still followed the same nighttime habits that she'd been doing for years. After she shut off whatever she was watching on television, she washed her face, brushed her teeth, and then spent about a half hour reading. She inevitably fell asleep with her glasses either on top of her head or in her hand. For her, reading was her transition to sleep, and she had been doing it for years.

As we saw earlier, having a regular bedtime routine works wonders for children. How would it feel to try something similar as an adult? This is a time for self-discovery and self-care. Use your personality to help you establish some routines that make you feel good. You can try some of the techniques in Chapter 4 that work with your senses. Scents, music, meditation, stretching, or even playing a game on the computer may help you relax. Drinking a cup of soothing tea or hot broth may be helpful for you. Reading a book for pleasure in whatever genre you like is also a great way to relax your mind. See if you can carve out a transition time before going to bed.

Create a Sleep-Conducive Environment

Sometimes bedrooms turn into much more than their original purpose. In addition to the place we sleep they can become an additional storage unit, an exercise studio, a kids' playroom, and a home office. Our beds can get covered with books, papers, animals, and clothes. It becomes harder to associate our bedrooms with relaxation. I asked Wendy Flynn, a feng shui consultant, for some tips on how to set up the bedroom so that it is conducive to sleep. According to Wendy, "Feng shui is the art and science of creating harmony within a living space. Feng shui was founded over five thousand years ago and studies the environment, people, places, time, and how they all work with one another." Feng shui is used throughout the world, including the United States, by many businesses that design both the interior and exterior of their buildings to create financial success. I often have been drawn into a store or appreciated a building because of the entrance or the layout within. Maybe feng shui explains why certain stores or restaurants in particular locations seem to fail more often than others. Perhaps there is something uninviting or nonflowing about their location. It gives us something to think about, but for now let's concentrate on how to create a more peaceful, harmonious atmosphere conducive to sleep in our bedroom.

When I consulted with Wendy, she said, "Balanced feng shui in the bedroom is fun and pleasurable for a quick nap, a good night's sleep, or to connect to that special someone." She said, "If you are having trouble sleeping, ask yourself these questions: Do you like all the items that surround you in your bedroom? When you wake up in the morning, do you feel happy with what you see? Before falling asleep, do you feel 'cocooned' and 'nurtured,' no matter with or without a partner?" If you did not answer yes to Wendy's questions, take a look at her tips that follow and use them to guide you.

Wendy's Feng Shui Tips

- Eliminate clutter: Make sure the bedroom is clutter-free and create a clear entryway to your bedroom.
- Separate work and sleep: Create separate areas for sleeping and for working. Sleeping is passive and working is active, so they should not share the same room.
- Create the right mood: Create a heavenly mood with soft background music when you go to sleep and when you wake up. Make sure your ears have enough downtime for the rest of the night.
- Provide good lighting: Use good lighting in your bedroom. Have a dimmer switch to adjust the energy accordingly. Good, appropriate lighting is very important, as light is important for general good health and one of the strongest manifestations of energy.
- Use calming colors: The right colors achieve a good feng shui balance in your bedroom. A feng shui bedroom has a balanced decor that promotes the best flow of energy for healthful sleep. Choose balanced colors in your bedroom so you have more energy after sleeping. Place stronger colors on your covers and pillows.

- Buy a good bed: A "good-looking" and well-balanced bed is very important in creating a perfect feng shui bedroom. A good mattress, a solid headboard made of wood and/or upholstered, and quality sheets from natural fibers are very important in creating harmonious feng shui energy.

I know from my work with the body-mind connection that we can sense when things do not feel right. You will probably know right away if your room is set up for sleep by using your mind-body connection to gather information about how things feel in your bedroom.

Finish Eating Well Before Bedtime

For many of us, it has become normal to work late and eat even later. You balance your schedule and your children's schedules, sometimes feeding them first and then yourself. We eat a heavy dinner too close to bedtime or relax from our day by snacking mindlessly in front of the television. Unfortunately, this causes many of us to go to bed on a full stomach. In addition, as we learned from our nutrition consultants, if we are worried, our ability to assimilate our food is affected or can cause us to choose foods that do not support our health.

I happened to meet a gastroenterologist a few years ago, and we ended up talking about all the medications being advertised for indigestion these days. He told me that in the United States over the past twenty years, there has been a rise in digestive issues. He said that because of the long hours Americans are keeping and the stress they face, they end up eating many of their meals later than previous generations would eat their dinner. He said he had seen more cases of acid reflux, in which the digestive juices of the stomach are washed up into the esophagus. This happens because we are lying down while our food is being digested. This affects our ability to sleep deeply and can create other health issues. For a better night's sleep and healthy digestion, leave a space of at least two or three hours between when you eat and when you go to sleep.

Exercise Regularly

Previously, we looked extensively at how exercise and movement can release worry. There is another added benefit. Regular exercise can help you sleep. Whether we work out in the morning, when our children are in school, or after work, physical movement helps us relax (as discussed in Chapter 5). Sometimes doing something simple like taking a casual walk after dinner with your dog, friend, or significant other will help your mind and body let go of the day's worries.

Most times, it is better to have some downtime after strenuous movement so that our bodies are not overly alert when we go to bed. High-intensity exercise, which causes our heart to pound and increases our metabolic rate, is the opposite of what our body needs for sleeping. Look at some of the suggested forms of movement toward the end of Chapter 5 to help with sleep. The more we can match our movement with our emotional needs, the more support we give ourselves when it comes to rest. If we can leave our worries behind through our choice of exercise, we create more of an opportunity to get a good night's sleep.

Avoid Caffeine Near Bedtime

As we saw in Chapter 6, excess caffeine raises our cortisol levels and has a strong effect on our nervous system. According to the National Sleep Foundation, caffeine remains in the body on average from three to five hours and can still affect people up to twelve hours later. When we are worried, we are usually walking around with enough nervous energy and tension to spare. Add in caffeine and we ramp up those sensations even more. As a big coffee fan, I know this is true. There used to be a time when I could drink anything with caffeine late into the evening, but now I definitely feel it linger in my body if I have it too late.

As dietitian Martha McKittrick mentioned, ingesting some caffeine can give us energy, but too much just makes us feel agitated. Further, I think it adds an extra layer of confusion to what we may be feeling. Because caffeine can mimic some of the symptoms of panic, such as a rush of energy and a rapid heartbeat, it is important to separate the real symptoms of anxiety and panic from the effects of caffeine. I often recommend that my patients who are experiencing anxiety or panic eliminate or reduce their caffeine intake. Then we can figure out the true level or baseline of their upset. Caffeine may affect us differently, but if we are having trouble sleeping, it is one of the easiest things to cut back on.

Avoid Alcohol near Bedtime

The pros and cons of the effect of alcohol on our health are constantly being debated. For many people, having a drink to unwind is part of a regular routine as long as there are no issues with abusing alcohol. When people describe the impact of alcohol, they often say, "It takes the edge off." That relaxing effect is very tempting when we are struggling with sleep. When alcohol enters our bodies, the potency of whatever we are drinking causes our bodies to respond quickly and move into an altered state. The illusion is that we are relaxed, but the reality is that something else, namely alcohol, is causing that sense of looseness. Eventually that feeling will leave, and we are left with the residue of alcohol. Most times alcohol disrupts sleep rather than enhancing it because it inhibits you from going into a deep state of sleep. When this happens, you wake up more easily but cannot return to sleep. The ripple effect of this is less quality sleep, fatigue the next day, and the aftereffects of excess sugar from the alcohol in your system.

Rest for the Weary

Besides sleep, I wanted to include some other ways we can recharge that have to do with rest. When we rest, we provide ourselves with the space to rejuvenate our bodies, clear our heads, and have a mini-break from worry. Of course, rest means different things to different people. My favorite form of rest is napping. I come from a family of nap takers, and we all love taking a snooze in the afternoon if possible. Those naps range from twenty minutes to an hour, depending on my schedule. My husband is just the opposite. Naps do not make him feel refreshed and in fact make him feel out of sorts when he wakes up. My friend Clara likes to sit out in her backyard when she needs to rest, simply looking at her flowers and drinking tea.

I believe resting involves shifting from an active state to a more passive one. When we rest, we acknowledge that we are human and not machines that can be productive every minute of the day. We need to rest more often than we think we do. Sure, there are times when we have to make a deadline, finish a paper, or nurse a sick child through the night, but many of us are going full tilt these days with no recognition of what that does over time. We need to take breaks in order to keep some sort of balance in our lives. If we do not allow for some down-time, our bodies have a funny way of making it happen. That is when we become susceptible to illness or injury, which forces us to take that much-needed break.

My patient Sam is a lover of nature. During the time we worked together, he had a stressful job that required him to put in long hours. Fortunately, the corporation he worked for was located on a piece of property that bordered a wooded area. This company had also invested in landscaping by creating different paths throughout the grounds for its employees to use. Sam took advantage of these paths on many occasions. Whenever he felt he was getting tired from his day, he would take ten or fifteen minutes and head off down one of the paths. Sometimes he would just sit and look out into the woods. He told me it provided a much-needed break. During these moments of rest, he would see an assortment of birds, deer, and small animals. This provided him with a sense of happiness and peace, which he would then take back into the office.

How often do you allow yourself to simply rest? And if you did, what would it look like? Can you imagine napping, listening to some music, staring into space, or sitting in the park? What would it be like to just do nothing for a while? Try the following exercise and see if you can discover how you would like to rest your mind and body.

Take a Time-Out

- Close your eyes and let your hands rest comfortably in your lap.
- Slowly breathe in through your nose and out through your mouth. Do this four or five times and concentrate on taking slow, deep breaths.
- Let your breathing return to normal.
- If there were no obstacles and you could take ten or twenty minutes for yourself today, tomorrow, or later in the week, what would you like to do to relax?
- Picture yourself actually doing what it is that would help you rest.
- Now, take a moment and notice how your body feels right now as you imagine taking the time.
- Do you feel anxious about resting? What is in the way?
- Is it an old belief or an actual situation?
- What can you do to shift that anxiety? Take the action or get a reality check.

- If you notice that you feel good when you picture yourself resting, what steps can you take to make it reality?
- Take another few deep breaths and open your eyes.

Sleep Away

It can be tough to get quality sleep when you are traveling and away from your familiar environment. Being in an unfamiliar setting after a long day can make it difficult to unwind. Try some of the following tips to help prepare and relax you when you are away from home.

- Pack some earplugs—they come in handy for unexpected noise in hotels.
- Take along an eye mask to block out excess light.
- Bring some familiar music that helps you relax.
- Pack your most comfy sleeping outfit—familiarity will help you unwind.
- Make sure there are adequate pillows and blankets; fold back the bedspread and arrange the pillows as you have them at home.
- Air out the room, turn on the air conditioner or fan, and bring some circulation into the room.
- If you carry pictures of your family or friends or even your pets, take them out and put them at your bedside when you are relaxing for the night.
- Stretch or take a hot bath or shower to relax before bedtime. (You can use the exercises in Chapter 5 as well.)

Time-Out

We all need to take a break more often than we realize when the noise and stress of our lives become too much. Whether the phone won't stop ringing, the plane is delayed, or you are at the relatives' for a long holiday meal, sometimes you need a real time-out. In addition to some of the breathing tips you learned in Chapter 2, you can always pop on some headphones and listen to a piece of music that really helps you feel happy, relaxed, and energized. If you don't have your music with you, here is a quick tension reliever that has you use your breath-and-body partnership.

Time-Out Exercise

Find a place where you can be alone: Shut the office door, go into a bathroom, or sit in your car. (You can also do this on a plane, train, or subway.)

> On each hand, put the tips of your thumb and pointer finger together. As you slowly inhale through your nose, press your fingers together like you are pinching something or making the OK sign.
>
> Exhale through your mouth and let go of your fingers. It should feel like the tension between your fingers is released when you let go.

Now put your thumb and middle finger together on both your hands.

Inhale slowly and squeeze the tips of your thumb and middle finger together the whole time you are inhaling.

Exhale through your mouth and release your fingers.

Do this exercise for each finger and for more than one round if you need it.

Rub your hands together and let your breathing return to normal.

When we honor our need for rest, we recognize our limitations. In my experience, the more we connect with what we need in terms of sleep, rest, and downtime, the better we are able to handle worry. A rested mind and body is more capable of facing adversity than a depleted one.

The Three Cs

Calmness

Sleep is an important contributor to our overall health. Not only does sleep give us the opportunity to reset our internal systems, but we need sleep to function on a daily basis. When worry keeps us up at night, we need to address how we can support our bodies. We all have a rhythm to our energy and will experience times when we need to rest simply because we have reached our limit. The more you can notice how your body operates and give it time to recharge when it needs to, the better you will be able to handle your worries. In addition, knowing that certain factors such as establishing routines for sleep, timing your meals, and creating a soothing atmosphere can improve your sleep will help you make those changes as well.

Clarity

As Dinah Washington, the jazz and blues singer, famously sang, "What a difference a day makes, twenty-four little hours, brought the sun and the flowers, where there used to be rain." She is absolutely right. Sleep involves resting your body and resting your mind. Many times when we have a decision to make or a problem to solve, we are told to "sleep on it." Something about the sleep process loosens the grip our minds have when we are stuck on a problem. When you feel your mind tumbling into the night, take the time to clear some space. You can write out your concerns, store them for the night, or talk them through with a trusted friend. Leaving your worries for the evening often provides clarity in the morning.

Community

If you are struggling with a longtime pattern of no sleep, it is important to find out what the physical, mental, and spiritual reasons may be. This is the time to research and use all the different resources that are available. You can start with your doctor or a psychotherapist or explore the support of a holistic practitioner. You can consider other experts who can help with stress relief, such as a massage therapist, acupuncturist, fitness professional, or nutritionist. You can also, as we have seen in this chapter, have someone help you with the physical layout of your bedroom. Get recommendations from colleagues, friends, and all the organizations out there that promote healthy sleep. Sleeplessness is not a new field of study, so there are many places to get good information.

We have delved into specific areas to target when you are handling worry. Movement, nutrition, and sleep are the cornerstones of good health. Each one can contribute greatly to how you look at the world and manage the variety of stress we all have in life. Now it is time to look at who is in your life, how you are spending your time, and what, if anything, your finances have to tell you about worry.

CHAPTER EIGHT

People, Places, and Things

Throughout this book we have looked at different ways to reduce worry. Achieving calmness by connecting with your body, getting clarity by tracking when and how worry shows up, and reaching out to a variety of resources have been the guiding principles for dealing with worry. In addition, good nutrition, moving your body, and getting enough sleep have a large effect on how we handle the worries in our lives. The more we can support our body, mind, and spirit, the better we will feel. The added benefit is that even if you are not experiencing worry at this time, you can still use the techniques for an improved quality of life.

I've observed that who we hang out with, where and how we spend our time, and how we handle our finances contribute greatly to our state of mind. I can still remember catching a television interview with the actor Gene Wilder and how his inspiring interview improved my mood. Before watching the interview, I was feeling overwhelmed and anxious about stuff to do and whether I would get it all done. Though some would have argued that procrastinating by watching the hourlong interview wasn't a good idea, I felt energized and ready to take on my tasks after hearing Gene talk about his acting journey. I remember noticing the difference and thinking, *Why? Why had my mood shifted from worry to motivation?*

I believe it was for two reasons. First, I gave my mind a break from the worry cycle I was in and let myself focus on something else. I had not planned on it, but I happened to catch the promo on television and became interested. I saw that it was not a serious or emotionally heavy show that would add to my worry. I chose to watch something that was light and easy to follow. This would allow my thoughts to shift from what I was worried about and give me the opportunity to concentrate on something else. As I have mentioned throughout this book, giving our thought patterns a break can help us reset the way we view the world. I was able to do this by watching an interview, which was very enjoyable. After it was done, I felt ready to face what I needed to with more clarity and energy.

I'm pretty sure my mood also shifted because I like and respect Gene Wilder as an actor, and in this interview he shared some personal information about the struggles he had gone through in his life. He revealed many things about how he became an actor that I had not known before. Despite many struggles, he had achieved professional success and was content in his personal life. He shared in the interview that he had needed emotional help at certain points along the way. The effort he put into getting to know himself contributed to his career. Because he allowed himself to evolve as a person, he evolved as an actor. As I listened, I remember thinking, *Well, if he can do it, I can do it.*

Have you had moments like that yourself? Times when you saw, heard, or witnessed someone who had overcome great obstacles to accomplish what they set out to do? I know I have, and they are not all famous or well known. They are friends, family, colleagues, or members of our communities who have been willing to keep going despite overwhelming odds. They became inspirational to us because of their perseverance. They radiate an internal confidence and have an outlook on life that just feels good to be around.

In this chapter, we will look at who supports and inspires us, where we spend our time, and what our relationship is with money. All of these areas, if out of balance, will contribute to or cause us worry. Cultivating people and being wise about the amount of activities you can handle will either add to or detract from how you view your life. The same holds true for how you are dealing or not dealing with your finances. Having these areas match up more to who you are and what you need will keep you from feeling out of control and burdened by excess worry.

Worrywarts

When my friend Daniel heard I was writing this book, his response was, "I come from a family of worriers. My mother worries, my grandmother worries, and so do all of my aunts. When I was a kid, whenever I wanted to try something new or go someplace different, my mother was always concerned about the danger. I know it was her stuff, but I definitely have inherited those tendencies. I have to keep on top of myself so that I don't hold back. I tell you, it's a hard habit to break." I asked him how he did stay on top of it, and he said, "I usually have a talk with myself and then make myself do what I want to do. Sometimes I listen to music or play some sports, anything to get me out of that mind-set." Daniel knows he has to fight against his mother's voice in his head.

The next time you are bothered by the nagging voice of worry, help yourself break free of it by having a firm talk with yourself. Remind yourself that even if you don't believe it right now, the nagging voice is not accurate or even rational. Give yourself permission to ignore it, as you have in the past, and then take some of the following actions to disrupt it.

- Put on your favorite song and sing along.
- Play your favorite piece of music and dance or play your air guitar.
- Wash dishes.
- Walk around the office.

- Vacuum.
- Take a walk.
- Go to the gym.
- Walk to your mailbox.

The people with whom we spend time from an early age onward influence our thinking and behavior. If, as in Daniel's case, you had a parent who worried over your personal safety, chances are you will have the same tendency. If you had a parent or parents who were more relaxed, you probably carry some of that with you when you are faced with a stressful situation. Sometimes we rebel against what we learned, but a lot of the early information gets in. We learn as children by watching and listening, regardless of whether the messages are verbal or nonverbal. We have seen in previous chapters that the behaviors of others who are older and more in charge have a powerful impact on us. Later in life, we choose to live our lives by shedding what no longer fits from childhood. This is what adulthood is about. As we continue to grow, we can either perpetuate those early influences or create new ones by becoming aware of whom we spend time with.

The Company You Keep

A September 10, 2009, article that appeared in the *New York Times Magazine* asked the question, "Is happiness catching?" In the article, a group of people in Framingham, Massachusetts, who were part of a heart study, were found to influence each other's health in a positive way. Two scientists, Nicholas Christakis and James Fowler, looked beyond just the health benefits of the study and found that whom we spend time with has a big impact on us in other areas as well. The article reported, "The Framingham participants, the data suggested, influenced one another's health just by socializing. And the same was true of bad behaviors—clusters of friends appeared to 'infect' each other with obesity, unhappiness, and smoking."

The word *infect* jumped out at me and seems to fit in with our focus on worry. In all sorts of environments you can find groups of people who are looking at life in either a positive or negative light. Whether they are at the office, your children's school committee, professional associations, or the gym, there are always pockets of people who like to worry. In fact, you rarely hear anything else from this type of person other than what is going wrong. They are usually the ones who, nine times out of ten, will answer "How are you?" with their latest worry. Their reasons for worrying may be very real, yet they cannot seem to shift from a gloom-and-doom perspective no matter what suggestions or support they receive. They may be carrying some old negative beliefs about the way life is, as we have talked about in earlier chapters, or may simply like to complain. Whatever the reason, the amount of time you spend listening to and participating in that kind of energy, the more you will be affected. Making conscious choices about whose company you keep can affect the way you handle your own problems.

We have discussed working with the Three Cs throughout

this book, and they are especially helpful in managing our personal relationships. If you find yourself choosing or hanging out with people who are constantly negative and see everything as a worst-case scenario, chances are good that you are going to increase the amount of time you spend feeling anxious and worried. There is a real difference between having people you can share your concerns with and people who are trapped in a cycle of complaining and fretting. Spend time with the second group and eventually the prism of your life will get cloudy and dark as opposed to having a clear vision. You usually can feel the difference between people who are chronic worriers and those who are not. If you feel better after spending time with them, even if there is no immediate answer to your worry, then those are healthy relationships. If you feel worse and end up with even more to worry about, then those are not supportive encounters. Using the Three Cs can help you figure out whether your relationships help you feel calm and relaxed, clearer about how to handle your worries, and supported in your community with information and care.

Besides our own perspective, getting a little outside feedback on our relationships can be illuminating. Sometimes we fall into the habit of spending time with people who infect us with their worrisome moods and views. After a while we adapt to that energy and start behaving the same way. Emily, a young woman in my practice, discovered this through feedback from her boyfriend. She was shocked by his reaction after a night out with a few of her friends from work. Emily's voice was incredulous as she said, "My boyfriend told me that all we did was complain and that it got to be really depressing listening to us!" She went on to say, "He said that now he knew why my mood was always so different after I hung out with these two. He said they were very negative people." "What about his remarks is so upsetting?" I asked. "I think he's right," Emily exclaimed to me. "But believe me, it took a big fight to admit it!"

Emily realized that her boyfriend had pinpointed a feeling she had dismissed within herself. She did feel less optimistic when she spent time with these two particular work friends and usually left their encounters feeling dissatisfied and pessimistic about her life. In moments like these, we can easily blame others for bringing our mood down, but we do have to examine why we are there in the first place. Is there something familiar and comfortable about the dynamic, like what Daniel experienced with his mother, who always worried? Are we hanging out with people who worry because of some old negative beliefs we have about our right to be happy? Are we perpetuating a cycle of worry without even realizing it? In order to help you figure out whether you are feeding or supporting a worry habit with the company you keep, look at the following questions.

What's Toxic/What's Not

- Find a place where you can sit quietly.
- Picture the people you spend time with (work friends, mom friends, best friends, dad friends, gym friends, church friends, etc.).
- Think about each category for a moment.

- Is there anything similar about the personalities in each group? What is it? Jot down the words that come to mind (funny, sarcastic, upbeat, dramatic, ambitious, complainers, etc.).
- Is there anything about each group that feels different?
- If you were to imagine that you were on your way to meet some of these people right now, how would you feel (excited, apprehensive, worried, happy, etc.)?
- Do these personal or professional friendships feel supportive or draining?
- Do you feel stuck or obligated to participate in any of these relationships?
- If so, how come?
- Finally, if for some reason some of the relationships would end, how would you feel (sad, relieved, anxious, free, upset)?

If you noticed that you would feel free and relieved if some of these relationships left your life, recognize that this is a key piece of information. Another quick way to gauge whether you are hanging out with a negative person or worrywart is to notice how you feel before, during, and after making plans with them.

Are you happy to meet them or not?

Do you feel good while you are there?

Do you walk away feeling that you had fun or spent quality time?

In general, you want to hang out with people who bring you support, wisdom, joy, and inspiration. Create time to be with them even if it is over the phone. If you do have to interact with people who are worriers and complainers, think about whom you can call and ask for support before or after the interaction. Think of all the people you can contact either in the moment or in advance so you do not get infected with worry. Keep a good balance of friends and make sure you have more in the "feel good" category than the other. If you do have to spend time with negative people, use the following tools to feel more in charge.

Subtle Things to Say When You Want to Change the Topic

"Okay, I've reached my 'life is terrible' limit for today. What else is going on?"

"I'll be right back." (Taking a physical break from the person or group you are with can help you feel less burdened by the energy. When you come back, change the subject as soon as there is an opening.)

"Great haircut (shirt, earrings, color) on you. I've been looking for something like that myself. Where did you get them?" (Use plain and simple distraction.)

Direct Things to Say When You Can't Indulge Negative Thinking

"To be honest, I know things have been upsetting for you for a while, but I need to take a break now from only hearing about the negative things in your life."

"Let's stop talking about this for now, because I'm starting to get really down and life is hard enough."

"You know, I find that when we get together, we spend a lot of time being negative. I'd like to change that. How about you?"

Breaking Up with a Toxic Friend

If you do have to end a friendship because it is toxic, is filled with drama, or no longer represents who you are today, you can choose to do so on your terms. You can have a heartfelt, respectful conversation explaining why you are choosing to end or take a break from the relationship. If you feel that is not possible, because the other person is too demanding or can't handle such a conversation, then breaking off contact and not being available is your other option. That means stating you're not free to meet and not returning calls, e-mails, or texts until the person stops contacting you. This draws a firm boundary and is needed in some cases.

Whom to Turn to and When

As I have dealt with my mother's diagnosis, I have needed to lean on a variety of people. My husband, of course, who witnesses the range of emotions I feel and manages not to get swamped by them. There has also been my younger brother Patrick, who shares the care of my mother with me. Many times we have passed back and forth our worry, words of comfort, and the insight needed to keep going. Other supports have been dear friends who listen with sympathetic ears and eyes. There have also been a surprising number of people, with whom I am not as close, who expressed words of care when they heard my news. I also joined an Alzheimer's group and have a place to talk about my worries with people who know exactly what I am going through. These are the types of relationships that keep us afloat when we are worried and scared. Not everyone can be there for us all the time, but if we have a variety of resources and know when we need to reach out, we can get through some very tough times. Think about the people in your life who can help you when you are worried. Be discerning about who can handle what types of feelings and information. As you may know, certain people are scared of emotions but are brilliant at strategizing. The opposite is true as well. Some folks are great with emotional support but not so skilled in helping figure out a plan. When we are worried, it is good to have a little of both types in our corner. Some of us may end up needing more formal support such as a group, a therapist, or spiritual counseling; others find solace with friends and family. Besides receiving support from others, keeping an eye on where we are giving our time will also keep us more balanced.

Learning to Say No

I have a feeling that most of your schedules are packed with activities that are important to you and your families. Whether you are taking your children to school, commuting to work, driving a parent to the doctor, or studying for an exam, you are probably super busy. I wonder, though, if we all sat down with our schedules, how much of our time would be balanced between what we want to do and what we feel obligated to do. *Obligation breeds worry, and, conversely, worry creates obligation.* These thieves of our time are often the reason we make decisions that are based on *should* as opposed to *want*. Over time, this can trap us with activities and events that keep us overly scheduled. How does this happen?

When we commit to doing something we do not want to do, we feel not only a sense of obligation but also the anxiety of knowing we have gone against our instinct. Instinctive feelings, which usually show up as sensations in the body, send us a signal when we are deciding whether we can take on something new. That signal is a feeling of either excitement or dread. If we go against that feeling of dread because we feel obligated, we not only end up having to complete whatever we said yes to but then have the added weight of knowing we didn't want to do it in the first place. Now, because we are overloaded, we have added pressure, which creates more worry.

So why don't we say no? For many people it is because they worry about the opinion of others and fear a negative reaction. They then find themselves agreeing to events, projects, and activities that they really do not have space for in their lives. Because they fear being judged or disappointing someone else, they end up saying yes. Many times people feel, because of early childhood experiences, that they do not have the right to their own needs. They may have had parents or guardians who were neglectful, distant, overwhelmed, or violent. When you grow up feeling that there is no space for your needs, you tend to put them last. These are needs that show up in both your personal and professional life. It's interesting that many people report having the instinct to say no, but the word gets stuck in their throat. Such a tiny word carries so much authority and so much anxiety. If you can learn to say no, you will have a powerful tool for reducing the amount of worry in your life.

When No Creates Yes

When did you last have the time to check in with yourself to see what you most needed on a body, mind, and spirit level? Many of us are continually on the go, which causes us to lose sight of what we need to take care of ourselves. We say yes to people and projects we do not have time for. We volunteer our time and energy, eager to help others at the cost of ourselves. We bypass our own needs in order to be nice or because we feel guilty about saying no. The more we overextend ourselves, the more we feel the effects. We notice that we feel a little wiped out or disorganized. We may feel tired and cranky because the hectic pace we are living eventually takes its toll on our bodies.

PRACTICING "NO" PHRASES

Learning to say no allows us to say yes to the things we really want. I understand, though, that it can be hard to say no if we are not used to doing so. I recommend two different strategies to get started. The first is the "I will have to get back to you" strategy. This is a buffer strategy that will give you the space to see if you really want to do something. We never want to feel rushed or pressured into a decision if our initial feeling is not a definitive yes. I understand there are times when we have to be quick on our feet, but most times it is best to really check in if we struggle with saying no. Whenever anyone asks if you can volunteer your time, take on a project, have a playdate, or meet for coffee and it is not something that your livelihood depends on, try using the "I will have to get back to you" strategy. Then once the buffer has been created, you can decide whether you want to take on that activity.

SOMEONE: Can you please feed my cat next week while I'm away?

YOU: I'll have to get back to you because I am not in front of my calendar and can't tell you what my week looks like.

After you get the request, sit with it for a few minutes and imagine doing what you have been requested to do. Picture the activity, favor, project, or meeting in your mind's eye. Think about your schedule and be realistic about the time you have available. Ask whether you are taking good care of yourself if you take on this request. If you feel you do not have the time, the answer is no.

YOU: Sally, I did check my calendar and unfortunately I won't be able to take care of your cat while you are away.

Remember, less is more; you are not obligated to state why you cannot do something unless you feel that the information is important for your boss, family member, or close friend to understand.

Strategy number two combines emotional truth with a firm no. When you have to say no to someone and you feel nervous about it, use the honesty of those feelings to help you. For example, you could say, "I feel bad that I can't help out, but it is too much for me right now," or "It's hard to say no to such a worthy cause, but I have too much on my plate at this time. I know you understand what that is like." Using this strategy allows you to get used to setting boundaries without having to force the word *no* out of your mouth. When you set these boundaries, you will have room for what you really need to focus on. The more you say no, the more you can say yes to what you really want.

Here are a few examples.

Example 1

SOMEONE: We would love for you to organize the spring festival, because you are a great events planner.

YOU: That's so flattering, but I'm afraid that the months leading to the festival are my busiest and I can't make such a commitment.

SOMEONE: But we could really use your help.

YOU: I understand, and it's hard for me to refuse such a request, but I have to at this time. (Tell the emotional truth but hold firm.)

Example 2

SOMEONE: I wanted to know if you could lend me some money to make my rent this month.

YOU: Unfortunately, that's not something I can do right now.

SOMEONE: But I really need the money.

YOU: I'm afraid you'll be upset with my answer, but it still has to be no. (Express your emotional truth—"I'm afraid"—and still say no.)

Remember, no one has the right to yell at you or berate you for not doing what they are requesting. If they do, you can give one warning and then get off the phone or leave wherever you are. For example:

SOMEONE (loudly): You know, I always knew you were stingy. I can't believe you won't give me this money. I know you have it!

YOU: My answer is no. If you don't stop yelling, I am getting off the phone (leaving the room, etc.). We can talk later when things are calmer. (Give your warning and then follow through.)

Body Truth

Each time we have to make a decision, we can use our body and mind's response to help us understand whether we *really* want to do what we are contemplating. This means becoming aware of the sensation of feeling drained and overwhelmed versus feeling energized. As we saw in Chapter 2, we probably will notice when we are overextending if our physical body, psychological perspective, or behavior patterns start to shift. Now is the time to start asking, what activities do we *want* to participate in and what activities do we *have* to participate in? Make sure there is good balance between the two. If not, a cycle of worry can start to happen or become worse. This is what happened to my patient Megan.

Megan was a woman in her early thirties, married, with two elementary-school-aged children. As most moms do, she had a very busy schedule, and she also worked as a writer. Megan initially came to see me for help with goal setting. During our work together she realized she had another big problem, and that was with overscheduling. She had been asked to head a committee at her daughter's school to raise money for a sports program. Though Megan felt uneasy about accepting the position, she agreed to do so. She later told me she felt she could not say no because she felt too guilty to do so. When I asked her why, she shared that though she was active in her children's schools, supporting them in activities and volunteering time, she never felt she gave as much as the other mothers. I asked her what she based this on, and she said, "I don't know. Everyone else seems so eager and willing to do anything for their children, and I never feel like I am giving enough. Since I work as a writer, I feel my time is not as flexible, and I feel guilty about that." Megan was comparing her insides to everyone else's outsides. She based what she was feeling about herself—not giving enough—against what others looked like they were doing on the surface, which appeared to be giving without hesitation.

Megan based her decision to be on the school committee on her belief that she was not giving enough and not on whether she really could handle the position with her current schedule. When we make these kinds of decisions, without determining whether it really works for us, we inevitably run into trouble. Trouble means we feel pressure, we get sick, or other areas of our lives begin to unravel. Megan discovered that to be the case. Between heading up the committee, meeting her writing deadlines, and managing her children's schedules, she was worried all the time. After the school project was complete, Megan smiled ruefully and said, "I will never do that again. I am still recovering." As with Megan, sometimes an unpleasant experience is the only way we find out about the impact of overextending. If we want to avoid learning lessons the hard way, we can start using our body more as a gauge and see if we feel anxious or calm when accepting an invitation to participate. Megan felt uneasy when she was first asked, but she allowed her guilt to override her instinct.

If this is something you struggle with, it is important to raise your awareness of how much energy you are expending in different areas. Reducing stress and worry means finding out what matters and what you can handle going forward. This means taking stock of where you want to spend your time and refocusing on your priorities. How do you get started? My suggestion is to take time to notice your true response to potential decisions and to continue to review what you need to feel more in charge. A great question to ask yourself is, "Does this work for me?" while paying attention to your body. The more attention you pay, the more information you will get. Here is a checklist that can guide you in your decision making.

Does It Work for Me?

- Try not to make any decisions when you are stressed, pressed for time, or tired.
- Before saying yes, use the "I will have to get back to you" strategy.
- Sit down and check in with your body.
- Think about the decision you have to make. Ask yourself, "Does this work for me?"
- Imagine yourself taking on whatever you have been asked to do.

- What do you notice physically when you picture yourself actually scheduling the time and then participating in that activity?
- Do you feel energized or drained? Sit with that feeling for a few minutes.
- What are the reasons you feel either energized or drained?
- Imagine saying no and see what you notice.
- Let both your body's response and your mind's knowledge inform your decision.
- If saying no directly is hard, link it with the truth of why you cannot commit at this time.
- Express your regret and feelings of being overextended or overscheduled, but hold firm on your decision not to participate.
- Notice how it feels to have more time and space to do what is important for you or your family.

Learning to carve out more time and setting boundaries is an ongoing process. Though we think we want to achieve perfect balance in our lives, the truth is life balance is more like a seesaw. We will have times of ups and downs filled with worries and concerns. The trick is to keep noticing how we spend our time and whether it includes our true desire to be there. Speaking of spending things, let us take a quick look at the connection between worry and money.

Financial Worries

I have found in my private practice and in life that no matter what the economy is doing, people worry about money. I am not surprised because we need money to live, to care for our needs, and to take care of others. Yet how we view money is a tricky thing. I have known patients with obvious wealth who worried about money and those with less who did not. I have seen people spend money to alleviate uncomfortable feelings and others who deprive themselves of any kind of spending. My observations about money and worry are based not on an accounting background but rather on a psychological one. In my view, money and emotional security go hand in hand. The more internal fear and worry we have, the more it affects our relationship with money.

There are many reasons for money concerns, and often they are based on real issues. We struggle with job loss, unexpected expenses such as health costs, moving, and the ups and downs of the economy. During times of economic strife it is so important to stay calm, get clarity about the steps we need to take, and tap into as much community as possible. I encourage my patients to focus on taking the small steps needed to handle big economic shifts because it can be overwhelming to focus only on what is looming in front of them. When we feel we have control in our lives, even in small ways, we feel empowered. When we feel empowered, we can take the next step and then the next step after that. Slowly, we move toward stability by keeping our focus on what we need to achieve financial stability. However, our beliefs about money reveal the most secrets.

Money Beliefs

Unconscious beliefs about money have surprising consequences. What we feel about spending, saving, and having is all tied into what money represents or will provide for us. Some people have a scarcity mentality and think there is never enough: enough money, possessions, or financial security. This often drives them to either overwork or barely get by with the minimum. They fear losing what they have, so they overcompensate with work or hold on to what they have even if they are underpaid. For those in the latter category, this creates the inability to make decisions that would better them financially. This can have disastrous effects when outside economic change happens, such as when rent, mortgage, or insurance payments rise. If we have been underearning and not allowing for more than "just enough," we can find ourselves struggling when the unexpected happens.

Another way that money worries show up is through unconscious spending. Unconscious spending can take the form of buying unnecessary items every time we shop because it makes us feel secure, or going on spending sprees. Unconscious spending sprees involve the urge to shop because of some mood we are feeling and then shopping to feel better. I have known patients who had clothes they never wore or bought in bulk to make sure there was enough. Both types of unconscious spending are about managing worry and anxiety. The act of buying or shopping unnecessarily provides both a distraction and a release. The need for distraction could be for many reasons: an unhappy relationship, an unfulfilling career, the loss of a parent, or a general sense of anxiety. The release from these feelings occurs with the anticipation of buying something, the search for the item, and then the actual purchase itself.

I had a patient many years ago who was deeply lonely and yet scared to be in a relationship. After being hurt by a previous boyfriend, she found herself withdrawing from social functions and potential dates. Most nights, after work, she found herself wandering from store to store buying clothes and cosmetics. She told me, "I never really use everything I buy, but I need somewhere to go and something to do." Luckily for this patient she had a job to pay for her purchases, but the items themselves never seemed to fill the hole in her heart. Over time, as her hurt healed, she was able to venture more into activities that involved her creativity and not her wallet. She discovered a love of hiking and joined a local hiking group. She later reported that she found the outdoors much more soothing than the shopping bags she used to bring home.

When money is used to relieve emotional tension, the relief is only temporary and the urge to spend begins again. Because the spending of money is not addressing the real root of the worry, the cycle repeats. We feel worried, and we find ourselves out spending to make it better. We spend, and it provides temporary relief but does not alleviate the real reason for being tense, so we spend again. However, if not enough money is coming in to cover what we are buying, another set of problems starts to emerge. Now maybe credit-card debt is created, a mortgage payment is missed, doctor visits are skipped, and the extra worry about all those things kicks in.

This kind of emotional spending can turn into an addiction, in which the urge to spend becomes overwhelming and out of control. This behavior occurs when our financial security and that of those we care for become compromised by debt and secrecy. If you feel you are in this category, professional counseling and twelve-step programs such as Debtors Anonymous are good places to turn.

One other way that money worries show up is in how someone feels about their self-worth. *Self-worth* is the way we value our abilities, innate talents, and general sense of self. I truly believe that money and self-esteem go hand in hand. If we have a poor opinion of ourselves, money is an area where that opinion can show up. I have had patients who did not value themselves and got rid of money as soon as they received it. They could not save or hold on to money because they did not feel they deserved it on some level. Sometimes they were not even aware of this pattern and could only recognize that they never seemed to have enough to cover their bills. Their finances were tied up with old negative beliefs. These beliefs, as we talked about in previous chapters, were either taught or absorbed through nonverbal behavior. For example, if you were emotionally neglected as a child, you might grow up believing you are unlovable. If you are unlovable, you do not deserve to have good things, including enough money. So when you have to earn it, either you get rid of it as soon as you can or you overwork and are underpaid. Both keep you from having more than just the minimum, the way you emotionally felt growing up.

In order to understand and relieve our worries about money, we need to give them our attention. How we do that will be based on what we are looking for and how we take in information. Do you need to be inspired? There are many books by people who started from humble beginnings and now are successful. Check out your library, bookstore, and online book retailers for their stories. Do you need the basics on money? There are books and classes on topics such as balancing your checkbook and making investments. Look to your community, local government, and business associations for classes and lectures. Do you need to understand more of your emotional relationships with money? There are therapists, coaches, and ministers who specialize in money issues. Ask friends, trusted colleagues, and employee assistance programs for referrals. Look around because there are lots of resources and lots of solutions. In the meantime, look at the following questions to start raising your awareness about your relationship to money.

Money Talk

- What words do you associate with money (happiness, fear, security, excitement, etc.)?

- Growing up, what were the messages you remember hearing about money ("Money causes unhappiness," "Be humble," "Do you think money grows on trees?")?
- What do you notice in your body when you think about the current state of your finances (fluttering in the chest, tightness in the jaw, lump in the throat, etc.)?
- Do you have a sense of what those feelings mean?
- What, if any, are the blocks you have around money?
- What needs to change?
- Do you believe it is possible?
- What do you need to make the changes you want?
- Where can you get that information, support, or guidance?
- What is one step you are willing to take to get what you need?

Finally, start telling the truth to yourself and those around you. How much can you really afford to spend? Take the financial pressure off and be realistic about where and on what you can spend your money. If you cannot afford to buy gifts, go to dinner, or travel right now, be truthful. Most people understand that there are times in all of our lives when we need to be frugal. Quality time spent with people you like and love is as valuable as any expensive thing you may buy. The more you can let go of what you imagine others will think and notice how they really behave toward you, the less worry you will carry.

Look at the following financial tips that can help reduce your worry about finances.

- Tell those you are closest to that you are on a money diet and will be cutting back on expenditures.
- Ask them for emotional support while you take care of your financial issues.
- Inform family and friends in advance that you will not be spending money on presents during the holidays so that you can stay on track financially.
- Instead, offer gifts of your time for babysitting, running errands, or preparing meals.
- Leave your credit cards at home and use cash only.
- Post your financial goals near your computer to stop you from late-night online purchases.
- Go to the library and get a basic money-management book on how to reduce debt and save money. Authors such as Suze Orman, Julia Cameron, and David Bach have a variety of books on how to work with your money issues.

The Three Cs

Calmness

We have looked at the importance of having harmonious and supportive relationships, making decisions that free up our time, and reducing anxiety concerning money. In all of these areas, we are looking to trust more how we feel in our bodies when we are choosing the people, places, and things in our lives. As we consider each area, we should think about whether we are feeling happy, content, and fulfilled. Remember, changes, even small ones, can cause shifts for the better in our lives. Think and feel your way through the decisions you have to make going forward.

Clarity

When you start to examine these three areas, you may be surprised at what you discover. If you have been feeling out of balance, worried, stressed, or overwhelmed, you want to understand why. When we do not have quality relationships, we are drained. When we are overextended, we feel frazzled. When we are stressed about money, our worldview shrinks. Regaining clarity in these areas requires self-examination. In order to feel that you are making the best decisions you can, take a good look at where your time and energy are going. Keep clearing out the pockets of stuck relationships, unnecessary activities, and issues around money that keep you worried.

Community

Our community is made up of people we spend time with and resources we turn to when we need information. The community of people we call our friends will be a special group, and we should feel good with them. Separate out how you want to spend time from a sense of obligation. The same holds true for your personal time. Give your time where you want and need to, but remember to include how you feel in your decision-making process. If you are struggling with financial issues, reach out to your community of resources and find the help you need. Professional support, online groups, classes, and books can provide the information you need.

CHAPTER NINE

Moving from Worried to Wellness

Reducing and managing our worry is an ongoing process. How could it not be? Our lives will always have a mixture of joys and sorrows, filled with events that will either elevate us or cause disappointment. This simply is the flow of life. However, having more control and techniques to weather the times when things do not go our way will enable us to stay grounded. I feel that managing worry is very much like running a marathon rather than a sprint. At times the effort and energy required for the journey will be overwhelming and draining. Therefore it is crucial to keep refueling and recharging your body, mind, and spirit as you go along, in order to take the next steps. How you do that is what this book is all about.

We have focused on supporting the body, mind, and spirit throughout each chapter. As you look over the checklists and exercises, you will notice the ones you are drawn to along with some you may have never considered. Keep using your body-mind connection and the instinctive messages you are getting about which techniques to try. You may start with one thing and shift to something else. You may try an exercise and have it morph into your own personal version. Remember how we looked at taking a break from "breaking news"? That is exactly what my friend Tara did when she was going through a particularly difficult time in her personal life, but she did it in her own way.

Tara had lost her mother to a devastating illness and understandably was very upset. She reacted the way that anyone would to that kind of loss and was in a state of grief. Even though she knew what she was going through was normal, she worried whether she would ever feel better again. After feeling very low for a period of time, Tara felt she needed to start actively working on raising her spirits. She decided to do this in her own unique way. She told me that she made a conscious effort at the end of the day to watch only old, classic sitcoms that were funny. She programmed her VCR, and after a long day she would climb into bed and watch them before falling asleep. Tara purposely fed herself a diet of humor in order to have something to counterbalance the grief she was feeling. Even when she felt that she would never feel better, she took this action anyway. She told me that it really gave her relief from her worrisome thoughts and helped greatly during a time of deep pain. Her choice illustrates how you can take many of the suggestions in this book and make them your own.

Sometimes we doubt very strongly that we can break free from our loop of worry or that anything we do will make us feel better. We feel weighted down with concerns and are skeptical about ever having a better frame of mind. I understand this and have been there myself. We are only human, and when we have been battered around enough by our worries and fears, it can sometimes be hard to believe that anything will help. At some point or another, we all reach our limit. At those times, we have to make a decision. Either we remain in our pain, which is certainly a choice and sometimes the only one we want to make, or we do something I call "Fake It Forward."

Fake It Forward

Fake It Forward means using one of the many techniques or strategies in this book or taking one from your own experience that has worked for you in the past. Fake It Forward means trying something even if you have zero faith, in that moment, that anything is going to help you feel better. In other words, you are going to fake your way into taking an action that will help shift your mind-set. Even if you have lingering doubts about your abilities or feel skeptical about the outcome, faking it forward means you are going to try it anyway. This requires you to use both your body and your mind. Your mind will be saying, "Oh, this is not going to work and why am I even going to bother?" while your body is literally moving you toward some kind of action.

When I was caring for my mom, I knew that I would need periodic breaks in order to recharge my energy. Because I love to exercise, I made a conscious effort to go to a local gym to relieve my stress. However, I found it hard at times to leave my mom, even though I knew she would be all right and in no danger if I did. I continually had to Fake It Forward to get out the door to go exercise. What I inevitably found was that as I drove to the gym, feeling tense and worried, something would change. I would feel my tension start to lift as I concentrated on the road and gave myself the break I needed. Of course, working out helped my stress enormously, and by the time I returned I was always in a better frame of mind.

When we are trying to Fake It Forward, we have to remind ourselves that it has worked in the past. Knowing what has made or will make us feel better is a good place to start. Here is one final exercise for you to try to help keep you from becoming worried sick. (Take a quick read of the exercise before you try it.)

Fake It Forward

Close your eyes, take a deep breath, and simply sit for a few moments.

Now picture the area of your life where you need the most support.

Ask yourself what one thing you need in the next week to help you feel more balanced or revitalized.

What do you need to jump-start the process?

Is there an action you need to take?

Do you need reassurance, information, or to form a plan with someone you trust to complete the action?

Where or from whom can you get what you need?

What is the one step you will take?

By when will you take it?

How does your body feel when you imagine achieving that action?

Take a deep breath and open your eyes.

Self-care is the key to managing your worry. Having a foundation of good health and mental clarity will keep your feet firmly on the ground when you are dealing with difficult issues. My personal and professional experience has shown me that having your body, mind, and spirit in the best shape possible is vital. I truly believe there are ways to keep from becoming sick with worry, and I wanted to share with you some of the things I have seen make a difference. Having witnessed so many transformative experiences as a therapist and as a woman, I know it is possible to keep going when we have the supports in place. I encourage you to take the time you need to care for yourself and I offer you my best wishes for living the fullest, healthiest, and most fulfilling life you possibly can.

S.A.N.E.

S STOP

Stop whatever you are doing for a minute, five minutes, or even an hour. Simply give yourself the space to catch your breath and take a break from what you are doing.

A ACKNOWLEDGE

If you are feeling out of control with food or drink, acknowledge that something is going on in your life that is causing you to cope by overdoing it. When we consciously think about our actions, they become choices as opposed to something happening *to us*.

N NORMALIZE

Normalize the fact that you have chosen food to manage your emotions and stress. Instead of beating yourself up, recognize that you, and many others, choose the same coping mechanism.

E EVALUATE

As you become aware of what you are feeling and how you are responding to it, you can evaluate what you need. This allows you to address whatever you are worried about using more long term solutions.

HEALTH AND WELLNESS RESOURCES

Professional Services and Support

I wanted to include a section clarifying some of the professional support services that can be used to dispel worry. You will find specific information on the experts consulted in this book along with information on some national organizations. Here, too, I wanted to provide you with some other options for when you feel you may need more professional assistance. These are only a handful of the many resources out there to use. Remember to ask people you trust for recommendations as well.

Psychotherapy

Psychotherapy is a process of exploring the issues, problems, and traumas that keep you from living the life you want. You can get psychological support from a variety of professionals such as licensed clinical social workers, psychologists, psychiatrists, family therapists, art therapists, dance therapists, or certified drug and alcohol counselors. The approach of each therapist will be different, and it is important to find someone experienced and supportive along with a personality and approach you feel comfortable with.

Hypnotherapy

Hypnotherapy helps you connect to inner resources so that you can let your conscious mind take a "rest" from negative self-talk and let the unconscious mind direct you toward positive self-talk and encouragement instead. Hypnotherapy moves you into a state of deep relaxation and often feels like deep meditation.

Emotional Freedom Techniques (EFT)

Emotional Freedom Techniques is an emotional version of acupuncture in which you stimulate the *meridian points*, which are energy pathways in the body, by tapping on them with your fingertips. Specific issues such as worry, stress, and anxiety can be targeted using this method.

For more information:

www.emofree.com

Eye Movement Desensitization and Reprocessing (EMDR)

Eye Movement Desensitization and Reprocessing (EMDR) is a comprehensive, integrative psychotherapy approach. It contains elements of many effective psychotherapies in structured protocols that are designed to maximize treatment effects. These include psychodynamic, cognitive-behavioral, interpersonal, experiential, and body-centered therapies.

EMDR is an information-processing therapy that uses an eight-phase approach to address the experiential contributors of a wide range of pathologies. It attends to the past experiences that have set the groundwork for pathology; the current situations that trigger dysfunctional emotions, beliefs, and sensations; and the positive experience needed to enhance future adaptive behaviors and mental health.

For more information or to find an EMDR therapist: www.emdr.com

Alzheimer's Association

The Alzheimer's Association is the leading voluntary health organization in Alzheimer's care, support, and research. Their mission is to eliminate Alzheimer's disease through the advancement of research; to provide and enhance care and support for all affected; and to reduce the risk of dementia through the promotion of brain health.

For more information:

1-800-272-3900

www.alz.org

The American Council on Exercise (ACE)

The American Council on Exercise is a nonprofit organization committed to enriching quality of life through safe and effective exercise and physical activity. Founded in 1985, today ACE is one of the largest fitness certification, education, and training organizations in the world. ACE currently has more than forty thousand certified fitness professionals in 107 countries. ACE certification, continuing education, and training programs are among the most respected in the fitness industry.

For more information or to find a trainer in your area: www.acefitness.org/findanacepro/default.aspx

Association for Spirituality and Psychotherapy (ASP)

ASP is a membership organization committed to the study of how psychotherapy can foster the emergence of the spiritual dimension in our lives, and how spiritual practice may enhance our personal lives and the psychotherapeutic experience. Drawing from all religious and spiritual traditions, psychological perspectives, and scientific theory and research, ASP emphasizes how the individual can awaken to spiritual traditions and practices.

For more information:

www.psychospiritualtherapy.org

Foundation for Human Enrichment— Trauma Healing

The Foundation for Human Enrichment (FHE) is a nonprofit educational and research organization dedicated to the worldwide healing and prevention of trauma. Somatic Experiencing (SE) is a body-awareness approach to trauma being taught throughout the world. SE restores self-regulation and returns a sense of aliveness, relaxation, and wholeness to traumatized individuals.

For more information or to find a Somatic Experiencing practitioner in your area:

www.traumahealing.com

Insight Meditation Society

Founded in 1975, the Insight Meditation Society (IMS) is a 501(c)(3) religious nonprofit organization. IMS is a spiritual refuge for all who seek freedom of mind and heart. They offer meditation retreats rooted in the Theravada Buddhist teachings of ethics, concentration, and wisdom. These practices help develop awareness and compassion in ourselves, giving rise to greater peace and happiness in the world.

For more information:
www.dharma.org

Institute for Applied Meditation (IAM)

IAM is a nonprofit spiritual school founded by Puran and Susanna Bair that develops and applies Heart Rhythm Meditation for integrating physical, emotional, and spiritual life to consciously create love, harmony, and beauty. Their books, *Living from the Heart* and *Energize Your Heart*, are full of practical information and exercises to develop heart health physically, emotionally, and spiritually.

For more information:
www.appliedmeditation.org

National Association of Social Workers (NASW)

The National Association of Social Workers (NASW) is the largest membership organization of professional social workers in the world, with 150,000 members. NASW works to enhance the professional growth and development of its members, to create and maintain professional standards, and to advance sound social policies.

For more information or to find a social worker:
www.socialworkers.org

The American Massage Therapy Association (AMTA)

The American Massage Therapy Association represents more than fifty-eight thousand massage therapists. AMTA works to establish massage therapy as integral to the maintenance of good health and complementary to other therapeutic processes and to advance the profession through ethics and standards, continuing education, professional publications, legislative efforts, public education, and fostering the development of members.

For more information:

www.amtamassage.org

The American Dietetic Association (ADA)

The American Dietetic Association is the world's largest organization of food and nutrition professionals. The ADA is committed to improving the nation's health and advancing the profession of dietetics through research, education, and advocacy.

ADA members represent a wide range of practice areas and interests including public health; sports nutrition; medical nutrition therapy; diet counseling, cholesterol reduction, diabetes, and heart and kidney disease; vegetarianism; food-service management, hospitals, restaurants, long-term care facilities, and education systems; education of other health-care professionals; and scientific research.

For more information:
800-877-0877
www.eatright.org

National Sleep Foundation

The National Sleep Foundation (NSF) is an independent nonprofit organization dedicated to improving public health and safety by achieving understanding of sleep and sleep disorders, and by supporting sleep-related education, research, and advocacy.

For more information:
www.sleepfoundation.org

Experts Consulted for
Worried Sick

Kelly Brogan, M.D.

In addition to general adult psychiatry, psychopharmacology, and psychotherapy, Dr. Brogan provides consultation and treatment of patients with medical illnesses and related psychiatric symptoms. Dr. Brogan also has experience in the treatment of women at all stages of the reproductive cycle experiencing mood and anxiety symptoms, including premenstrual dysphoric disorder (PMDD), pregnancy and postpartum symptomatology, and menopause-related illness. Those with an interest in holistic or integrative medicine and herbal/nutraceutical supplements will find that Dr. Brogan is a knowledgeable resource for treatment considerations.

For more information or to contact Dr. Brogan:
646-706-7771
kellybroganmd@gmail.com
www.kellybroganmd.com

Jeanette Bronée, CHHC, AADP

Jeanette Bronée is a nourishment counselor and certified Ericksonian hypnotherapist. She works with health from an integrative functional medicine point of view. She is an integrative health counselor who is board certified with the American Association of Drugless Practitioners (AADP) from the Institute of Integrative Nutrition. She has been educated in macrobiotic healing and is also certified as a compassionate integration counselor in the Tom Monte Method. In her Path for Life Self-Nourishment Center she teaches how to achieve healing through food choices while integrating the emotional healing and behavioral shifts that need to take place for a truly integrated new relationship to food, self, and life.

Her approach to food is educational, upbeat, and nondogmatic. She loves being both the Sherlock Holmes of health to find the root cause of the symptoms and the change motivator for each individual client to uncover what is holding them back from healing and changing their habits for good.

For more information or to contact Jeanette:
212-260-0604
jeanette@pathforlife.com
www.pathforlife.com

Jane Burbank, LCSW

Jane Burbank is a licensed psychotherapist, well-known singer, performer, and voice teacher based in New York City. In addition to psychodynamic therapy, Jane specializes in pet bereavement, offering support and counseling for those who are experiencing loss connected with a pet.

For more information or to contact Jane:
212-592-8970
jane@janeburbanklcsw.com
www.janeburbanklcsw.com

Tina Felluss, LCSW

Tina Felluss is a licensed psychotherapist, workshop leader, and certified Nia instructor in New York City. She uses movement to help her clients connect with the deeper parts of themselves. Her practice specialties are spirituality, body awareness, and life after cancer.

For more information or to contact Tina:
212-662-3850
tina@tgfelluss.com
www.tgfelluss.com

Wendy Flynn, Feng Shui Consultant

Wendy Flynn is an internationally known compass school feng shui master and has been helping to transform homes and businesses since 1994. She is trained in design, sales, and management in the fashion industry. She studied with several different masters while learning feng shui. She has worked with architects, builders, and interior designers and given consultations and lectures at major corporations, banks, federal agencies, and realty companies. Wendy provides feng shui consultations worldwide for residential and commercial properties. She has made numerous television appearances, and her work is featured in local, national, and international newspapers and magazines.

For more information or to contact Wendy:
530-925-0826

Leigh Hansen, BA, LMT

Leigh Hansen is a licensed massage therapist and the founder of Remedy Massage Therapy in New York City. Leigh and her team specialize in using therapeutic massage techniques to meet the specific and often changing needs of each client. Their work has brought relief and rejuvenation to those suffering from stress, injuries, chronic health conditions, and everyday aches and pains.

For more information or to contact Leigh:
212-604-4745
leigh@remedymassage.com
www.remedymassage.com

Tara Keegan, CCA, HHC

Tara Keegan is a certified clinical aromatherapist, a board-certified holistic health counselor, and an energetic healer. She has developed Connective Healing, a holistic approach to health encompassing nutrition, energy medicine through the meridians, the chakras, and neurolymphatic points. To rebalance and realign the human body and spirit ultimately helps clients connect to their higher mission and find peace and balance in life. Tara specializes in women's health, stress management, and addiction challenges. She lectures throughout the United States and supports individual clients in New York City, Washington, Florida, Ireland, and the Caribbean.

For information or to contact Tara:

718-414-5130

tckeegan@gmail.com

Martha McKittrick, R.D., CDE

Martha McKittrick is a registered dietitian and certified diabetes educator in New York City. She specializes in weight management, diabetes, heart health, sports nutrition, PCOS and women's health issues, as well as preventive nutrition. She is known for giving practical and realistic advice. Martha is also a speaker, writer, and spokesperson.

For more information or to contact Martha:

212-879-5167

mmckitt@aol.com
www.martha-nutritionist.com

Rochelle Rice, MA

Rochelle Rice is a nationally recognized speaker, author, and educator. She dedicates herself to empowering women of size by connecting the body, the mind, and the heart through focus, movement, and breath. She is the author of *Real Fitness for Real Women* (Warner, 2001).

For more information or to contact Rochelle:
212-689-4558
rochelle@rochellerice.com
www.rochellerice.com

Reverend Amy Torres

Amy Torres is an interfaith minister, spiritual teacher and counselor, and Heart Rhythm Meditation instructor based in New York City. She helps people gain self-awareness by using their bodies and relationships as a classroom to identify and transform their unconscious beliefs into an ongoing state of inner peace.

For more information or to contact Amy:
212-340-1201
www.amytorresacim.com